CAMBRIDGE LIBRARY COLLECTION

Books of enduring scholarly value

Travel and Exploration

The history of travel writing dates back to the Bible, Caesar, the Vikings and the Crusaders, and its many themes include war, trade, science and recreation. Explorers from Columbus to Cook charted lands not previously visited by Western travellers, and were followed by merchants, missionaries, and colonists, who wrote accounts of their experiences. The development of steam power in the nineteenth century provided opportunities for increasing numbers of 'ordinary' people to travel further, more economically, and more safely, and resulted in great enthusiasm for travel writing among the reading public. Works included in this series range from first-hand descriptions of previously unrecorded places, to literary accounts of the strange habits of foreigners, to examples of the burgeoning numbers of guidebooks produced to satisfy the needs of a new kind of traveller - the tourist.

Crozet's Voyage to Tasmania

Published in 1891, Henry Roth's translation of Crozet's narrative provided the first English account of the infamous French expedition to the South Pacific. The ship left France in 1771 under the command of Marion De Fresne (1724–1772). After exploring Tasmania (the first Europeans to do so), De Fresne's party set out for New Zealand, arriving shortly after Captain Cook. Crozet (1728–1782), took over command of the expedition when De Fresne and twenty-six crew members were killed and allegedly eaten by local Maori in the Bay of Islands. While much of the book is concerned with the exploration of New Zealand, Roth's translation begins with the origins of the expedition, the journey through the Pacific islands, and Tasmania and the discovery of people there, ending with descriptions of Guam and Manila. The work also includes a preface and discussion of the literature of New Zealand by James R. Boosé.

Cambridge University Press has long been a pioneer in the reissuing of out-of-print titles from its own backlist, producing digital reprints of books that are still sought after by scholars and students but could not be reprinted economically using traditional technology. The Cambridge Library Collection extends this activity to a wider range of books which are still of importance to researchers and professionals, either for the source material they contain, or as landmarks in the history of their academic discipline.

Drawing from the world-renowned collections in the Cambridge University Library, and guided by the advice of experts in each subject area, Cambridge University Press is using state-of-the-art scanning machines in its own Printing House to capture the content of each book selected for inclusion. The files are processed to give a consistently clear, crisp image, and the books finished to the high quality standard for which the Press is recognised around the world. The latest print-on-demand technology ensures that the books will remain available indefinitely, and that orders for single or multiple copies can quickly be supplied.

The Cambridge Library Collection will bring back to life books of enduring scholarly value (including out-of-copyright works originally issued by other publishers) across a wide range of disciplines in the humanities and social sciences and in science and technology.

Crozet's Voyage to Tasmania

JULIEN MARIE CROZET

CAMBRIDGE
UNIVERSITY PRESS

CAMBRIDGE UNIVERSITY PRESS

Cambridge, New York, Melbourne, Madrid, Cape Town,
Singapore, São Paolo, Delhi, Tokyo, Mexico City

Published in the United States of America by Cambridge University Press, New York

www.cambridge.org
Information on this title: www.cambridge.org/9781108030885

© in this compilation Cambridge University Press 2011

This edition first published 1891
This digitally printed version 2011

ISBN 978-1-108-03088-5 Paperback

CROZET'S VOYAGE TO TASMANIA

ETC.

CROZET'S VOYAGE

TO

TASMANIA, NEW ZEALAND

THE

LADRONE ISLANDS, AND THE PHILIPPINES

IN THE YEARS 1771–1772

TRANSLATED BY

H. LING ROTH

AUTHOR OF "THE ABORIGINES OF TASMANIA," "A SKETCH OF THE PEASANTRY
OF EASTERN RUSSIA," ETC., ETC.

WITH A PREFACE AND A BRIEF REFERENCE TO
THE LITERATURE OF NEW ZEALAND

BY

JAS. R. BOOSÉ

LIBRARIAN OF THE COLONIAL INSTITUTE

Illustrated

LONDON
TRUSLOVE & SHIRLEY, 143, OXFORD STREET, W.

1891

HERTFORD:

PRINTED BY STEPHEN AUSTIN AND SONS.

PREFACE.

Mr. HENRY LING ROTH, the translator and editor of this work, has brought before the public the complete narrative of an event which, at the period of its occurrence, attracted great attention throughout the civilized world. It is therefore the more surprising that, amid the numerous collections of Voyages and Travels published during the last century, this Voyage to the South Seas, full of interest as it is, has not received the full attention of the English translator until now. The discovery of a practically new hemisphere in the Southern Seas, and the progress of settlement there having been the theme of a long series of histories in the several languages of Europe, it is un-necessary to tread in so beaten a track by the recital of occurrences of which few can be ignorant; but at the same time no account of Australasian exploration would be complete without a general reference to the great work performed prior to the discoveries of the French, with which this work deals.

In the year 1642 an expedition was fitted out by the Governor-General of the Netherlands-India, Antony van Diemen, for the purpose of exploring the Coast of the Australian Continent, which had been sighted by previous adventurers, the command being entrusted to Abel Jansen Tasman. Entering the Pacific from the Indian Ocean, Tasman's energy was rewarded first of all by the discovery of land which, as the Navigator's Journal states, "had not before been known to any European, and was named Van Diemen's Land in honour of the Governor-General who sent us out to make discoveries." Tasman followed up this important discovery by sighting the coast of a mountainous country, which he named Staaten Land, in honour of the States-General of Holland, this being more than a century later named New Zealand by Captain Cook. It is generally acknowledged that after Tasman's there is no record of any other vessel visiting this part of the Southern Seas until the arrival of Captain Cook, who in 1769, after observing the transit of Venus at Otaheite, first sighted the Coast of New Zealand. Cook's explorations of that country far surpassed those of his predecessor Tasman; for whereas Cook took every advantage of coming into contact with the natives and gaining information with regard to the country, it is an admitted fact that Tasman never landed on the shores of New Zealand at all, contenting himself with sailing and anchoring off the coast. Cook's visit was undoubtedly the most important that has ever been made to New Zealand, if only the geography of the country is taken into consideration; and all other extracts from the accounts of explorers who followed up to the time of the settlement and formation of a European Government have added but little to the geographical information for which he is responsible. In fact, Cook himself states in the account of his first voyage, that the situation of few parts of the world is better ascertained than that of at least a portion of the coasts of New Zealand investigated by him; and in connection with the voyage treated of in this work, this statement is confirmed by the testimony of Crozet,

Marion's lieutenant, who says: "As soon as I obtained information of the Voyage of Cook, I carefully compared the chart I had prepared of that part of the coast of New Zealand along which we had coasted with that prepared by Captain Cook and his officers. I found it of an exactitude and of a thoroughness of detail which astonished me beyond all power of expression. I think therefore that I cannot do better than to lay down our track off New Zealand on the chart prepared by the celebrated English navigator."

Following closely in the wake of Captain Cook, and, in fact, having intercourse with the natives at the same time as the English expedition, was Captain de Surville, in command of the French vessel, *St. Jean Baptiste*. This explorer had been despatched from France on a secret expedition, which fitted out at great expense, and from which extraordinary results were anticipated. De Surville was, however, singularly unfortunate, and added little intelligence to the information then available with regard to the exploration of the great Southern Lands.

Having so far traced the course of discovery to the period of the visit of M. Marion du Fresne, the account of which, together with the report of Cook's Voyage, was the means of turning the attention of Europeans to the importance of those lands, which at the present time form one of the brightest portions of the British Empire, it may be well to refer to the issue of the work dealing with the results of Marion's Voyage. The first account of the expedition was published in Paris in 1783, under the title of "A New Voyage to the South Seas, commenced under the Orders of M. Marion." The work was compiled

and edited from the papers of M. Crozet by the Abbé
Rochon, himself a distinguished traveller, and appeared
under the privilege of the French Academy, the entry of
the book in the Academy's Register having been made
on the 11th May, 1782. Some doubts appear to exist,
however, as to whether or not a second, or even a
third, edition was subsequently issued. Opinions upon
the subject are varied, which fact renders it difficult
to arrive at a definite conclusion. Whilst it is upheld by
most eminent students of Australasian Bibliography, both
in England and France, that only one edition of the work
has been published, viz. that of 1783, it is strange that
in Professor Craik's work, entitled "The New Zealanders,"
forming one of the series of the Library of Entertaining
Knowledge, and published in 1830, it is stated that in
addition to the first edition, there appeared in 1791 a
volume containing an account of the Abbé Rochon's own
voyage to Madagascar and the East Indies, which was
reprinted in 1802, with the addition of two other volumes,
in the last of which appears a second narrative of the
voyage of Marion, in most respects copied from the former,
but with a few new remarks interspersed. Dr. Thomson,
the author of "The Story of New Zealand," published in
1859, in a bibliography relating to that country, which
forms an appendix to the work, refers to three editions
as having been issued. After comparing these statements
and inspecting the Abbé Rochon's work, there appears be
be no confirmation of the fact that the original edition was
ever reprinted—although extracts have in many instances
been embodied in various collections of voyages. It may
be that the authors of the two works above referred to

have been misled by the publication of the Abbé Rochon's works in 1791 and 1802, which contained the results of his own voyages.

The Voyage of Marion de Fresne, or Crozet's Voyage, as it is otherwise known, was performed during the year 1771, and is a modest account of the exploration of a party of Frenchmen which went in search of the great land which, in those days, was supposed to exist somewhere in the Southern Ocean. It embraces an account of the discoveries made in Van Diemen's Land and New Zealand, the various troubles the party met with, the massacre of part of the expedition, including the Commander, by the Maories, the sojourn at the Ladrone Islands, and the final arrival at the Philippines, all of which incidents are graphically described. If the book at the present day can hardly lay claim to a scientific character from a geographical point of view, it can confidently be recommended as one of surpassing interest.

In the translation the spirit of the French text has been strictly adhered to, and the explanations added by Mr. Ling Roth greatly enhance the value of the work. The results of the expedition affecting two important portions of the British Empire cannot fail to be of interest not only to every British subject, but more especially to the historical student. The former may care to learn something of the history of discovery in the Southern Seas, whilst the latter will, doubtless, find a deep attraction in tracing the origin of the formation of Colonies which, a century ago, kept alive a spirit of rivalry amongst the representatives of the British and of the French Nations.

J. R. B.

LIST OF PLATES.

LIST OF ILLUSTRATIONS IN THE TEXT.

    "The gentleman had an opportunity of seeing the operation of *amoco*, or tattooing, performed upon the face of a young man of Tekokee's tribe. He lay upon his back, with his head resting upon the knees of the operator, who sat upon the ground, and for whose guidance the intended form of the *amoco* had been previously traced in black lines upon the patient's face. The point of the tattooing chisel was about half a quarter of an inch wide; it was made of the wing-bone of an albatross, and fastened in a transverse wooden handle. Before each incision, the instrument was dipped in a calabash of charcoal and water, and then laid on the part and lightly struck with a bit of stick not larger than a common pencil. As the lines of the *amoco* became more contracted, a narrower instrument was used. Though the blood gushed out at every puncture, the patient bore the operation with perfect composure, and whatever the pain might have been at the time, the inflammation that followed and continued for many days was quite frightful." (Major R. A. Cruise, Journal, p. 136.) Owing to the inflammation of his face, the patient is unable to chew his food, and hence the necessity of feeding him on liquid food.

CONTENTS.

INTRODUCTION.

Origin of Expedition.—*Aoutourou.*—Marion du Fresne's family. —His career.—The astronomer Pingré.—L'Abbé Alexis Marie de Rochon and Kerguelen at the Mauritius.—Governor Poivre.— Lieutenant Crozet.—Captain Duclesmeur.—Result of collision between the *Mascarin* and *Castries.*—Rochon's view of the massacre.—Captain Cook's account of Crozet.—Assistance received in the translation of the work.

CROZET'S VOYAGE.

Bougainville's Taïtian.—Marion's offer to return the Taïtian to his country.—Arrangements made by the Governor of the Mauritius.—The Departure.—Death of the Taïtian at Madagascar. —Sail for the Cape.—Losier-Bouvet and *Cape Circumcision.*— Gonneville's lands.—The mythical islands *Dina* and *Marzevan.*— Van Ceulen's charts.—Cold weather.

DISCOVERY OF SOUTHERN ISLANDS:

Misty weather.—Land sighted.—The *Terre d'Espérance.*—Moss patches.—*L'île de la Caverne.*—The Marion Islands.—Collision between the two vessels.—Its result.—Foul weather.—The *Iles Froids.*—*Iles Arides,* and *Ile Prise de Possession.*—Crozet Group.

LANDING AT ONE OF THE AUSTRAL ISLANDS—OBSERVATIONS MADE ON THIS ISLAND:

Act of taking possession.—Snow.—Barrenness of island.— Tameness of the wildfowl.—Icebergs.

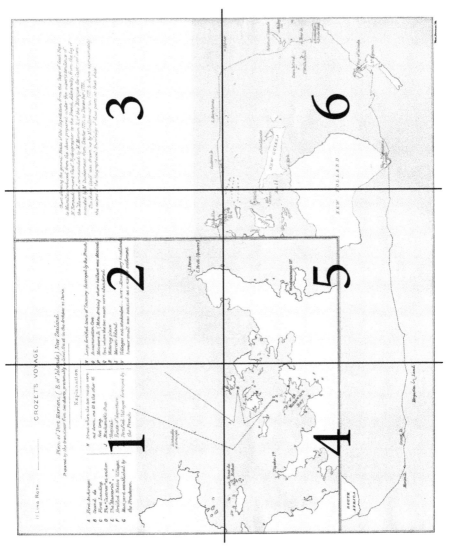

Key to following pages.

Plan of Port Marion, (B. of Islan

Prepared by the translator from two charts, presumably by

Explanation.

A	First Anchorage.	H	Forest where the two masts were
B	Second do.		cut down; one 65 & the other 45
C	First Landing.		feet long.
D	The "Castries" at anchor.	J	Blacksmith's Shop.
E	The "Mascarin" „ „	K	Hospital.
F	Fortified Native Villages.	L	Route of departure.
G	Mast yard established by	M	Fortified Villages destroyed by
	the Frenchmen.		the French.

N
0
P
Q
R
S
V

Sentinelle
& avancée

L

1

ds) New Zealand.
Lieut. Crozet in the Archives at Paris.

✓ Large fortified town of Tacoury destroyed by the French.
Assassination Cove.
Motouara Is. (Motu Arohia) where ballast was obtained.
Spot where the two masts were abandoned.
Watering place.
Marion Island.
✓ Villages not stockaded :— NOTE :—Almost every headland however small was occupied as a native settlement.

Chart sho
to Manilla, ˧
M. Renaud, p
the "Mascari
manded by ˧
The chart
the extent of

I. Percée
C. Brett (Quarre)

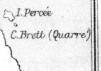

Manilla

nds) New Zealand.
by Lieut. Crozet in the Archives at Paris.

Chart sh
to Manilla,
M. Renaud,
the "Mascar
manded by
The char
the extent

N Large fortified town of Tacoury destroyed by the French
O Assassination Cove
P Motouara Is. (Motu Arohia) where ballast was obtained.
Q Spot where the two masts were abandoned.
R Watering place
S Marion Island.
V Villages not stockaded :— NOTE:—Almost every headland
   however small was occupied as a native settlement.

I. Percée
C. Brett (Quarre)

Manilla

owing the general Route of the Expedition from the Cape of Good Hope
reduced from the chart prepared under the superintendence of
present Chief Hydrographer to the French Admiralty, from the log of
in" commanded by M. Marion & of the "Marquis de Castries" com _
M. Duclesmeur, from October 1771 _ to December 1772.

t itself was drawn up by M.Duclesmeur in 1775 & shows approximately
f the Geographical Knowledge of these parts at that date.

Ladrone Is.
S. Bartolomeo

Guam

St Peter

3

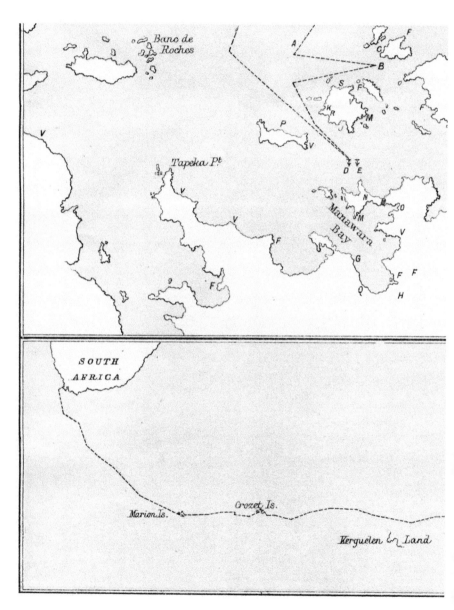

Banc de Roches

A

C

F

B

S F

K R V

M

P

V

D E

Tapeka Pt

V

V

N M O

S M

F

Manawara Bay

V

G

F F

Q

H

SOUTH AFRICA

Marion Is.

Crozet Is.

Kerguelen Land

4

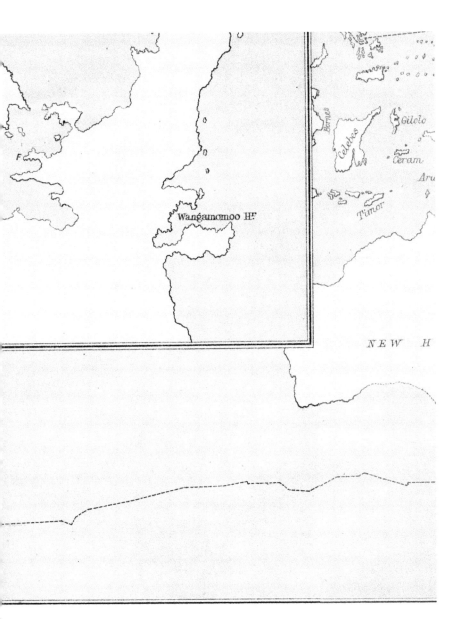

F

Borneo

Celebes

Gilolo

Ceram

Aru

Wanganomoo H^d.

Timor

N E W   H

5

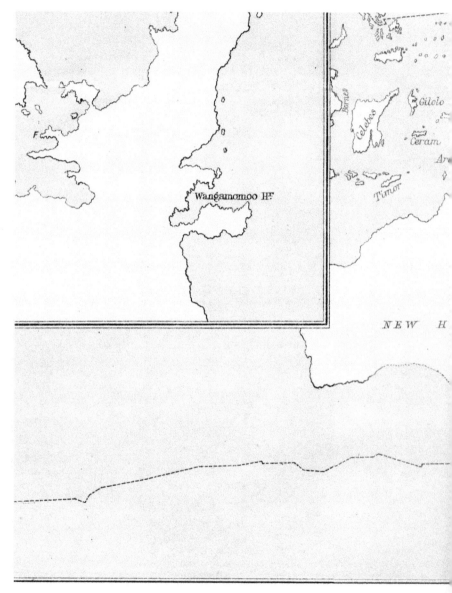

Wangamomoo Hr.

Borneo

Celebes

Gilolo

Ceram

Ar

Timor

NEW H

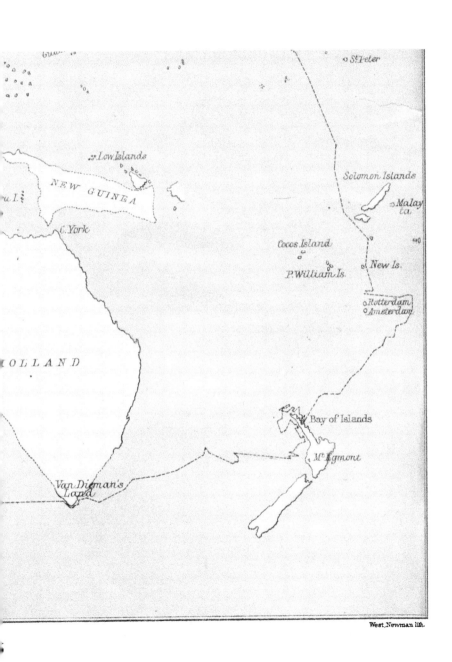

INTRODUCTION.

THE origin of the expedition described in this work was due to the desire on the part of the French Government to return to his native land a Taïtian, named *Aoutourou* (*Mayoa*), whom Bougainville had brought with him to Europe as a human curiosity in 1769. This South Sea Islander had been sent to the Mauritius together with instructions to the Governor of that French dependency to forward him to his destination. Marion du Fresne, the chief of the expedition about to be described, was then a well-to-do resident at the Ile de France, and he volunteered, as is related, to take *Aoutourou* to his home.

Nicholas Thomas Marion du Fresne was born at Saint Malo in 1729. His family is at the present day represented by the Boismena family at Saint Malo, and there is supposed to be a branch, name unknown, in Nantes. The following extract from the registers of the Etat Civil de Saint Malo, obtained through the kindness of the British Vice-Consul the Hon. E. Henniker Major, relating to his baptism is interesting:

"Nicholas Thomas Marion, son of Nicholas and of Jaquette Pilvesse his wife, was baptised by me, the undersigned, on the twenty-second of December, 1729. Jacques Poitevin was godfather, and Catherine Mathays was godmother. The godfather and father have signed:

JACQUES POITEVIN,
NICHOLAS MARION,
(Signed) F. PAIN, *Baptisavi.*"

Marion entered the French navy, became a lieutenant on a frigate in 1746, and a captain of a fire-ship in 1766. He was

also made a Knight of the order of Saint Louis.   Previously he
had commanded the vessel which took the celebrated astronomer,
A. G. Pingré (1711-1796) to Rodriguez island in 1760 to observe
the transit of Venus there.   Captain Marion was known as "an
extremely intelligent man, a good strategist, a good all-round man,
and one in whom implicit confidence could be placed."   It was
natural that a wealthy man with such renown would have his
offer graciously received by the Governor of the Mauritius.   At
the time the expedition was about to start the astronomer and
traveller Alexis Marie de Rochon was on a visit to the island.
He had gone there with Kerguelen to take part in the latter's
second voyage, but not agreeing with his views, he declined to
go further.   The Governor of the island, M. Poivre, at first wished
Rochon under the circumstances to go with M. Marion, but
afterwards, in hopes of reconciling Captain Kerguelen and the
Abbé Rochon, he positively refused the latter his permission
to start with M. Marion.   It is probable that to this circumstance
we are indebted for the published account of the expedition, for
Rochon edited it from the log of M. Crozet, one of the officers,
who took charge of the *Mascarin* on the death of Marion, and
who met with well-deserved promotion on his return to France.
Associated with Marion was an officer known as the Chevalier
Duclesmeur.   This man distinguished himself on his return to
Europe in the squadron under the command of Touche-Tréville.[1]

It was Captain Duclesmeur who assumed command of the
whole expedition on the death of M. Marion.   He was also, it
appears, wounded by the natives of Tasmania, and the way in
which he successfully withdrew the expedition from its dangerous
position at the Bay of Islands is greatly to his credit.   The great
object of the expedition, apart from that of returning the
wandering Taïtian, was the discovery of lands in the Antarctic
Ocean, but this object appears to have been brought to a sudden

---

[1] Vice-Admiral Touche-Tréville, born 1745, died on board the *Bucentaure*
19 August, 1804.   He commanded the *Hermione* in her successful withstanding
of the English frigate *Isis* in 1780; he was taken prisoner by Commodore
Elphinstone at the mouth of the Chesapeake in 1782, and taken to England.
He returned to France in 1783, and again commanded vessels successfully against
the English.

end by the unfortunate collision between the two vessels which formed the expedition. The *Castries*, which appears to have suffered most, although she afterwards occasionally outsailed her consort, has been blamed for being the cause of this change of view, but M. Rochon asserts that Marion must have had other ideas not known to us for so completely changing his original object.

In the appendix will be found M. Rochon's views of the massacre which cost Captain Marion his life, and which he attributes to hostile acts committed by the vessel commanded by M. de Surville. He adds : "The desertion of a negro belonging to Marion might have contributed to the rising of the islanders, already shocked by the flogging inflicted on one of their companions ; for although it is said that the savage who had stolen a sword out of the gun room went without punishment, Duclesmeur states the savage was put in irons and that his companions swam off threatening to wreak vengeance on Marion." Either cause may in itself have been sufficient to rouse the natives, or we may not be wrong in inferring that a severe breach of the "tabu" must have been the origin of the mischief, for these early voyagers appear to have known nothing whatever of that remarkable custom in New Zealand or elsewhere.

In the account of his second voyage Captain Cook says the account of M. Marion's expedition had not been made public in 1776, and "did not come to my knowledge in time enough to afford me any advantage." He had been told at the Cape by Baron Plattenberg, the Governor, in November, 1772, that Captain Marion had started, but that was all. On his return from his second voyage, March, 1775, he met Captain Crozet at the Cape and says of him : " He seemed to be a man possessed of the true spirit of discovery, and to have abilities. In a very obliging manner he communicated to me a chart, wherein were delineated not only his own discoveries, but also those of Captain Kerguelen. . . . . Besides this land . . . . Captain Marion . . . . discovered six islands which were high and barren. These, together with some islands lying between the line and the southern tropic in the Pacific Ocean, were the principal discoveries made in this voyage, the account of which we were told was ready for publication."

In this translation of Rochon's work there are many references to geology, botany, and zoology, which at the present day it is quite hopeless to attempt to describe correctly, and the editor is therefore all the more indebted to Mr. F. W. Rudler of the Royal School of Mines, to Mr. W. Botting Hemsley of Kew, and Mr. W. Eagle Clarke of Edinburgh, for kind help in the translation of respective technical details.

Of the two maps specially draughted for this translation, one, showing the general route of the expedition, has been prepared from Crozet's log, under the kind superintendence of M. J. Renaud, Hydrographer-in-Chief to the French Admiralty; the second one, showing the movements of the expedition in the Bay of Islands, where Marion was killed, the editor has prepared from Crozet's two charts in the Naval Archives at Paris.

In the selection of the Illustrations the editor is much indebted to Mr. Walter Clark, who has kindly placed at his disposal negatives of the plates of the articles illustrated from the Science and Art Museum, Edinburgh, and more especially to Mr. Ch. H. Read, of the British Museum, who has enabled him to lay before the reader a few illustrations of some of the choicest works of Maori Art.

CROZET'S VOYAGE.

In the course of his voyage round the World in 1768 and 1769, M. De Bougainville had brought to France a native of Taïty, an island in the South Seas. This Indian was the object of much interest in Paris on account of his frankness and of his excellent natural qualities. The Government sent him to the Isle of France with orders to the Administrators there to take measures to secure his return to his native country.

M. Marion du Fresne, the Master of a Fireship,[1] and a smart

---

[1] As a fireship is almost a thing of the past, and therefore almost unknown to the present generation, a short description of this class of vessel, kindly given me by Mr. R. C. Leslie, author of "Sea Wings," etc., will be of interest to the reader: "The fireship was certainly a distinct class of vessel in our navy as far back as 1684, and from Marion being spoken of as *lieutenant de brûlot,* there can be no doubt that the French (who in most things connected with the material of their navy were ahead of us) also had a class of vessel in their navy specially rated and fitted up as 'Fireships.' From a draught of one I have by me, these fireships were from 90 to 100 feet long, by 14 feet in beam, with a draught of 10 feet, and they must have been from 200 to 300 tons. They were armed with 20 guns upon a 'spar or uncovered upper deck like a corvette, while the main deck, or that which answered to a frigate's main deck, had eight ports on either side, besides one upon each quarter aft, much larger, and called the sally port, having two large upright doors opening outward. This large port was used as a means of escape by those of her officers and crew in their boat who remained on board until the last moment to sail her among the enemies' ships, and then to light the slow matches connected with powder trains, etc., by which the ship was set in a blaze, and ultimately blew up, scattering the combustibles, fireballs, and langrel shot, with which she was freighted, among the enemies' ships, which were mostly attacked in this way when anchored at night in an open roadstead. One very marked feature in the construction of these fireships was that the eight main-deck ports on each side were *let down* in place of opening *upwards* like an ordinary gunport, so that when open the port lid (Fig. 1) helped to conduct the flames, etc., in an *upward* direction,

sea-officer, seized the opportunity to distinguish himself by making a new voyage and by making discoveries in little-known seas. He offered to carry the Indian to his native country at his own cost. He asked for one of the King's storeships to be attached to his own vessel, offering to pay all the expenses of the expedition himself.

The Administrators[1] of the Isle of France advanced him the necessary sums for the armament of these two vessels, and M. Marion gave surety for the payment of these loans. Although by this arrangement the whole expedition came under the control of M. Marion, the Governor of the Colony gave him the fullest instructions concerning the lands he was to go in search of and on the physical and moral observations he was to make in the course of his voyage. It was proposed he should advance sufficiently to the south in order to try and discover the islands, or the continent, which it was supposed were to be found in this southern portion of our globe, the Governor of the Isles of France and Bourbon being particularly anxious that the most northerly portions of this supposed land should be discovered, as they

instead of towards the sea, as they would have done if hinged from above, like the ordinary gunport (Fig. 2). Fireships were also provided with what were

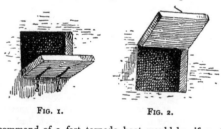

FIG. 1.   FIG. 2.

called fire-trunks or wooden funnels placed under the shrouds to carry up the flames to the masts and rigging. No doubt the command of these vessels was given to the smartest and most intrepid among the younger officers of those days, just as to-day the command of a fast torpedo boat would be, if sent upon a night attack upon a fleet of large ironclads."

[1] The Governor of the Isle of France was then Pierre Poivre, 1719–1786. He was a great traveller, and established the first French Agency in Cochin China. During his travels he was three times taken prisoner by the English, and on the decline of the Compagnie des Indes he retired into private life. From this retirement he was called away to govern the Mauritius, which post he appears to have fulfilled with the greatest benefit to the island, personally leaving the island as poor as he entered it. It was probably to his initiative that Marion's expedition was so anxious to collect new industrial plants for the Isle of France.

would be nearer to the colonies and under a more temperate climate than the more southern portions. He hoped they would find timber for masts, and a variety of necessaries which the Isle of France, so far distant from any chief seaport, could only obtain at the expense of great trouble and cost. The Governor pointed out to M. Marion that during the season which commences in November and ends in April it was impossible for the ships of the Isle of France to be employed usefully; that they had to be laid up in port, where they were not even safe from storms, and that they remained there at an expense to the colony; that this stormy season at the Isle of France was the most favourable for starting and exploring the southern lands, and that great advantage would accrue to the Isles of France and Bourbon from the discovery of these lands. M. Marion thoroughly understood the soundness of these views and desired most eagerly to acquire glory in making discoveries which he foresaw might give a new career to the colony in which he owned property.

FIG. 3.

The Court of France had just sent M. de Kerguelen[1] to the Isle of France with permission to visit this part of the world, and if possible to complete by his discoveries a knowledge of the earth in all its inhabited or habitable parts. It was important in order to carry out the views of the Court on this point to interest M. Marion in them, for he was leaving at a time of the year apparently more favourable than that in which M. de Kerguelen could depart,

---

[1] Kerguelen-Tremarec, 1734-1796. He was sent on two Arctic and two Antarctic expeditions, and in the course of the first of the latter discovered Kerguelen land. This land Cook afterwards re-discovered and was inclined to call it Desolation Island. Kerguelen was also sent by Louis XV. on a mission to England to report on naval construction. On his return from his second expedition he was charged with various indiscretions and imprisoned at Saumur. He left the Isle of France on 16th January, 1772, and on 18th October, 1773, respectively on his two Antarctic expeditions.

and who was moreover to attempt his discoveries by quite a different route.

In consequence of these arrangements, M. Marion chose the most experienced officers in the Colony, and he engaged me as one of them to ship as his second in command.

The native of Taïty, named *Mayoa*, embarked with M. Marion on the 18th October, 1771. The two vessels, namely the *Mascarin* commanded by M. Marion, and the *Marquis de Castries* commanded by the Chevalier Duclesmeur, first of all put into port at the Isle of Bourbon. The Indian was there attacked by small-pox, of which he had probably taken the germs with him from the Isle of France, where this epidemic was making cruel ravages at the time of the departure of the vessels.

For fear of introducing into the island a disease which is looked upon as almost as dangerous as the plague, M. Marion was obliged to depart from the Isle of Bourbon, and anchored in the Bay of Fort Dauphin in Madagascar, in order to let the disease run its course, and so as not to carry it with him to the Cape of Good Hope, where he was obliged to go in order to complete his outfit. However, on the morning of our anchoring in the Bay of Port Dauphin, the Taïtian died, and an affidavit recording his death was made.

The chief object of the expedition having thus become void by the death of the Indian whom we were to carry back to his native country, it would perhaps have been more proper under the circumstances to have taken the vessels back to the Isle of France, and there to have paid them off for employment in some other object. But M. Marion's desire to make useful discoveries, and to distinguish himself by a new voyage, overbore all other considerations.

We therefore started for the Cape of Good Hope, where in a few days we completed the provisioning of the two ships for an eighteen months' cruise. This being accomplished, we set sail from the roadstead on the 28th of December, 1771, and at eleven o'clock in the morning M. Marion directed his course towards the South in order to discover the Southern Lands.

This search had already occupied M. Losier-Bouvet, who in

1737 saw a Cape which he named *Cape Circumcision*. But the land discovered by this able navigator was apparently not the same where Captain Gonneville had touched in 1503.[1] The route followed by M. Bouvet indicated to M. Marion that he must look for these lands to the east of the meridian, which passes through Madagascar.

Nothing remarkable happened from our departure from the Cape of Good Hope until the 7th January, 1772, when our latitude observations showed us that we were in the parallel of the islands *Dina* and *Marzeven*. These islands are marked on the charts of Van Ceulen[2] in lat. 40 to 41, and I do not know why our modern hydrographers do not mention them, for they should not ignore that several Dutch vessels knew them thoroughly, and I have even been assured that these islands are well wooded and watered.[3]

Our longitude by reckoning was, on the 7th of January, 20° 43′ east of Paris. Next morning we saw a large number of gulls, and the sight of these birds showed us we were not far from the islands we have just mentioned. The sea had changed much: it was rough now with a violent wind. We left these parts on

[1] Binot Paulmier de Gonneville, a French navigator, who discovered some land never properly charted, and which was by the way also for a long time supposed to be a portion of Madagascar. He departed from Honfleur in 1503, returning with an Indian Chief's son named Essomeric. On his return he was captured by an English Corsair, and did not get back to France till 1505. His crew declined to return to the Indian's country with the chief's son, and it was a descendant of this Essomeric who in 1663 published in Paris an account of Gonneville's voyage. M. Margry lately made the discovery that the land visited by Gonneville was on the coast of Brazil. Bouvet de Losier, who was sent in command of the frigates *Aigle* and *La Marie* to search for Gonneville's land, discovered Bouvet Island (S. lat. 54° 50′, and E. long. Paris 4°) on 1st January, 1739 (not 1737). Captain Lindsay in the *Swan* saw the island in 1808, and Captain Norris of the *Sprightly* was the first to land there (16th December, 1825). The latter named it Liverpool Island, but which name it has of course not retained.

[2] Jean Van Keulen and afterwards Gerard Van Keulen were Dutch hydrographers, who were chiefly known by their excellent marine charts.

[3] With regard to these two islands, which only appear on Keulen's chart and have since not been heard of, it seems strange that so late as 1820 an English captain should have tried to make them. See p. 18, Goodridge's Narrative of a Voyage to the South Seas, London, 1832. It is, however, not at all improbable that these islands are identical with the Marion Group.

the morning of the 9th January, considering that the search for the Southern continent should alone occupy our attention. On the 11th I took a latitude observation, 45° 46'; the reckoning for the longitude was 28° 46' east of Paris. Although in the Southern Hemisphere the month of January corresponds to the month of July in the Northern Hemisphere, yet we experienced the severest cold in the height of summer and in a climate which appeared to be placed in the temperate zone. As snow fell almost the whole time we were in these parts, we could not attribute the cold we suffered to any sudden change of weather.

On the 12th January we saw some *poules mauves*,[1] gulls, sea-wolves,[2] and sea-weed. At six o'clock in the evening M. Marion sounded and at 130 fathoms there was no bottom. At eight o'clock in the evening we clewed the mainsail and continued during the night under the two maintop-sails and the fore-sails. The sea was fairly fine and the weather was foggy. I noticed that at sundown the gulls and other birds flew towards the east and east-south-east, a fact which announced lands in that direction.

DISCOVERY OF SOUTHERN ISLANDS.

At six o'clock in the morning of the 13th January we saw, returning from the west, gulls, *poules mauves*, and some other birds, which never fly far from land. We continued our east-south-east course and saw many sea-wolves and much sea-weed, with which the sea was covered. On sounding we found no bottom at 130 fathoms.

At two o'clock in the afternoon we were surrounded by a fairly thick mist and we also had some rain. The sea was fine and smooth, but there was a swell from the west. At four o'clock the wind freshened. We unreefed the main-sail and the sea once more changed. At half-past four we sighted land which extended four to five leagues from west-south-west to west-north-west. As the fog was thick and we might be mistaken, we sounded and found bottom at 80 fathoms, with coarse sand mixed

---

[1] Probably a variety of gull.   [2] Probably fur seals.

with coral. At the same time we saw also very clearly more
land to the north.

Continuing our course and following the bearing of the first land,
the centre of the middle portion of which was to the west of us, we
found we had coasted along it three leagues further during the
night: we had in fact followed its lay until we saw it behind us.
Before seeing it I had noticed that from midnight until four
o'clock in the morning, the sea had been smooth and calm, as
if it were sheltered by land, and was shallow. As soon as we
had sighted this first land, which now remained behind us, I
took bearings and hastened to sketch the view for fear that the
fog would not let us see it for any length of time. We only
saw about six or seven leagues of its side view, but we did not
see it end to the W.N.W. nor to the S.E., so that it is quite
possible this land may extend very far, and may possibly form
a part of a southern continent. The land appeared to rise
very high, covered with mountains doubled and trebled one on
top of the other. Suddenly the fog robbed us of our view.
M. Marion named it *Terre d'Espérance* (Land of Hope), because
its discovery flattered us with the hope of finding the southern
continent we were in search of. It was too foggy for us to
find out whether the country was covered with vegetation or
whether it was inhabited.

At the sight of these lands to the west and north, and all the
more as we appeared to see land towards the south-east, M.
Marion feared to be caught in a bay, and directed his course to
the north. The wind then rose and the sea became very rough,
and although we tried hard to pass this island to leeward, we
were ultimately forced to pass it to windward. Before the bad
weather set in I had taken bearings, and had drawn a sketch of
the island, the north-western portion of which we had not seen.
In sailing along this island I noticed a cove on its north-eastern
part, in which there appeared to be a large cavern; around this
cave we could see a multitude of large white spots, which in the
distance looked like flocks of sheep.[1] Had time permitted it,

---

[1] The *Challenger* noticed these spots, and found them to be large patches of
moss.

we thought we might have found anchorage opposite this cove. I believed I saw a waterfall coming down the mountains. In doubling the island we discovered three islets, of which two were in a recess formed by the shore, and the third was at its most northern point. This island appeared barren, and was about seven or eight leagues in circumference, and without vegetation, its shore fairly secure and without danger. M. Marion called it *L'île de la Caverne* (Cavern Island). These two southern lands[1] are situated in lat. S. 46° 45', and long. 34° 31' E. of Paris, and half a degree to the east of the route followed by Bouvet in search of the lands of Gonneville.

On the morning of the 14th January we returned to look for the first Land of Hope, which we had discovered the night before, and which the mist, together with the wind, had prevented us knowing better. We approached to within six leagues, and sounded again, finding bottom at 80 fathoms, with fine sand mixed with detritus of shells. On approaching the land, I noticed on its north-east side a cove formed by low and abrupt points. We were not sufficiently close to be able to ascertain whether this land was wooded: it was covered with mist, but it appeared very green to us; the mountains were very high, and the tops were covered with snow. These mountains are high enough to be visible at sea 12 leagues off. We were about to look for an anchorage in the cove before us, and to survey this land, when, while preparing to sound, our two vessels ran foul of each other. The *Castries* lost her bowsprit and fore-sails. We lost our mizen-mast, the taffrail of our poop, our starboard gallery, and several hen-coops. This accident quite upset our plans, but luckily the wind had fallen and the sea was now quiet. We sent three small masts to the *Castries* with carpenters to rig them up. The repairs occupied us three days, during which we had favourable weather, but the wind having then become very violent, we abandoned our discovery, and continued our voyage along the 46th south parallel.

I cannot help remarking here that the thick and almost con-

---

[1] This group of islands is now known as Marion Islands, and has been described in the *Challenger* Reports, Narrative, Vol. I. Part I.

tinued fogs which reign in these parts are a very great hindrance to those in quest of discoveries, and render navigation extremely dangerous, and considering the state of the *Castries*, we dared not venture further south.[1] Having seen the mountains of the Land of Hope covered with snow, it was most probable that a few degrees further south we would have been surrounded with ice, as was the case with M. Bouvet.

Since we sighted the first lands, which we were now leaving behind us, we met incessantly with kelp, gulls, divers, penguins, and sea wolves. Up to the 24th of January, when we saw some of the new lands, we had nothing but fog, rain, and excessive cold. These lands appeared first of all to be two islands and I drew a sketch of them eight leagues off; later on they looked like two capes, and we thought we could see that they were joined by land. A moment later fog and night deprived us of the view. They are situated in 46° 5′ lat. S. and in long. 42° E. of Paris by dead reckoning. M. Marion called them the *Iles Froids* (Cold Islands).[2]

We made little headway during the night, and keeping together, and in the same parts, proposed to make a better survey of the lands in the morning; but on the 23rd we lost sight of them. We had apparently wandered during the night, the weather being foggy and rainy, and we found ourselves in one of those currents which run strongly north and south.

The same day, 23rd January, we changed our course to the east. The *Castries*, which followed us, signalled that land was in sight. It turned out to be a very high island, which appeared to me to end in a big cape. I took bearings to E.S.E. at a distance of about ten or twelve leagues. We tacked about in order to get near to this land, but when we were about six or seven leagues off a thick mist came down, and, lasting about twelve hours, robbed us of the view. M. Marion did what he could in order to get near the land, but our crews could only work with difficulty on account of the continual rain and cold, for they were not sufficiently warmly clad to withstand a

---

[1] See Introduction.
[2] Now called Hog and Apostles Islands.

climate in which the summer is much severer than is the winter on the shores of France. A big iceberg which we saw on that day, at about five o'clock in the evening, can give one an idea of the cold we experienced.

At three o'clock in the morning of the 24th we saw again the same island which we had first discovered the previous day. There was little wind at the time, the sea was however rough, but it was less misty. M. Marion ordered us to approach it and circumnavigate it. I saw the island very distinctly at two leagues off. It was round and so high that in fine weather it could be seen 20 leagues off. The summit of the mountains was covered with snow.

At nine o'clock in the morning we perceived to the S.E. another island, which appeared to me even higher than the one along which we were coasting. This island was also round, more mountainous, but smaller than the first island; we called it *Ile Aride* (Barren Island). These two islands lie East and West of each other at a distance of about nine leagues from cape to cape. At eleven o'clock M. Marion had a boat lowered and ordered me into it in order to go and take possession, in the name of the King, of the larger of the two islands, which is situated in latitude 46° 30′ S. lat., and by reckoning long. 43° E. of Paris. M. Marion called the island the *Prise de Possession*. This was the sixth island which we had discovered in these southern regions.[1]

LANDING AT ONE OF THE AUSTRAL ISLANDS.—OBSERVATIONS TAKEN ON THIS ISLAND.

My first care on setting foot on shore was to deposit, according to custom, the bottle, which contained an account of the act of taking possession, on the top of a pyramid about 50 feet above sea-level and formed of large rocks piled one on top of the other. The spot where I landed was absolutely stony. I mounted an eminence from whence I saw snow lying in several

---

[1] This second group of islands is now known as the Crozet Islands, and has likewise been described in the *Challenger* Reports.

FIG. 4.—VIEW OF EAST ISLAND, CROZET GROUP, ENVELOPED IN MIST, SEEN FROM H.M.S. *Challenger*

valleys: the land seemed barren and was covered with a very fine small grass. I found several of those coarse plants which are called *ficoïdes*, very much like those which are so common at the Cape of Good Hope. On returning to the shore, I noticed a small rush resembling grass and some amaranthus; the rocks were covered with moss and lichens; the shore was covered with a sort of rush about a foot high, very similar to that which is found at the Cape of Good Hope. The sea-weed around the shore was of an extraordinary size and had very large leaves. I could not find a single tree or shrub on the island, and I did not remain long enough to find fresh water, but appearances seemed to indicate that it could be found in the valleys which I had perceived from the eminence I had climbed.

As this island is continually exposed to the ravages of the stormy westerly winds which blow throughout the year in these regions, it does not appear to be habitable. I only found sea-wolves, penguins, petrels, *envergues*, cormorants, divers, and every variety of aquatic bird which navigators meet with in the open sea when they double the Cape of Good Hope. These animals, which had never seen men before, were quiet and allowed themselves to be captured by hand. The female birds quietly hatched their eggs, others fed their little ones, and the sea-wolves continued their bounds and their games without seeming the least scared by our presence.

I was surprised to see a white pigeon, which had no doubt strayed from some neighbouring land, and it seemed to me one might well argue that we were not far off from a big country which produces the proper seed-food for this bird. Meeting with a very big iceberg in the middle of this temperate zone helps to support this opinion. The route taken by M. Bouvet could now no longer stand in the way of our looking for the lands of Gonneville in these regions. I have already observed that M. Bouvet after having discovered Cape Circumcision in lat. 55° was obliged to alter his course northwards and was unable to continue his search beyond the 32° E. of Paris. From this point he had gone northward to strike the Isle of France.

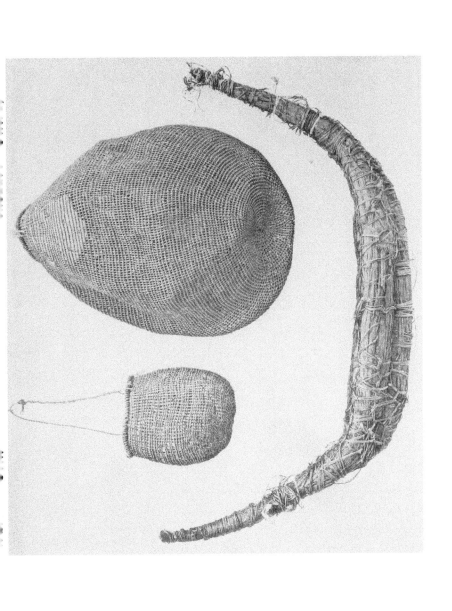

Our position was now favourable for the discovery of the southern continent if only we could have advanced in a south-easterly direction; but unfortunately the state of the *Castries* since she was dismasted did not allow M. Marion to follow out his otherwise well-matured plans.

CONTINUATION OF THE VOYAGE.

After leaving the island *Prise de Possession*, we followed latitudes 46° and 47°, and were in a continual fog, which was so thick that we were frequently obliged to fire off our cannons in order to save ourselves from collision. It frequently happened that we could not see the quarterdeck motions from the forecastle. Sea-weed, penguins, sea-wolves, and gulls with grey stripes were seen every day.

On the 2nd of February we were in lat. 47° 22′ S. and 62° long E. [of Paris], that is to say, 1° 18′ to the north of the southern lands (discovered on the 13th of the same month by the King's store-ships *La Fortune* and *Le Gros Ventre*),[1] and thirty-one days after our first discoveries in this part of the world. Had it not been for the accident to the *Castries*, we should have touched them more to westward, and there is every reason to believe that we would have found the lands seen by Gonneville, which must be more to the west and of easier approach than those seen by MM. de Kerguelen and de Saint Alouarn.[2] The sea-wolves, the sea-weed, the birds we saw every day, and the thick fog we met with when the wind was in the north, informed us of a neighbouring land to the south of our track. On the 10th February we were in lat. 45° 36′ S. by dead reckoning, in long. 81° 30′. On taking lunars I found we were nearly in longitude 90° E. of Paris. On that day we changed our course and directed our route towards the southern portion of New Holland known as Van Diemen's Land. We met with nothing remarkable until we sighted this country on the 3rd of March. I

---

[1] The land here referred to is Kerguelen Island, and the two ships named were those under Kerguelen's command.

[2] St. Alouarn was one of Kerguelen's lieutenants.

calculated we were then in lat. 42° 56′ S. and long. 146° 20′ E. of Paris.

The chart will give an exact idea of the track we followed until we anchored in the sound named by Abel Tasman *Frederic Henry Bay*, and which according to this navigator is situated in lat. 43° 10′ south.

Anchoring off Van Diemen's Land, Description of the Country, Observations upon its Inhabitants.

As soon as we had anchored, in 22 fathoms, on a grey sandy bottom, we lowered the boats and quickly perceived about thirty men seated on the shore. This part of New Holland[1] promised us much from the beauty of the landscape which met our view. From the fires and smokes which we had seen day and night, we inferred that the country was thickly populated.

The next morning the gigs and longboat were sent ashore armed, and some of the officers, marines, and sailors landed without any opposition. The aborigines showed themselves agreeable to our landing, collected firewood and made a sort of pile. They then offered the new arrivals some dry lighted boughs and appeared to invite them to set fire to the pile. We did not understand what they meant by this ceremony, but we lighted the pile; the savages did not appear at all astonished at this, and they remained round us without making either any friendly or hostile demonstrations. Their women and children were with them. The men as well as the women were of ordinary height, black, with woolly hair, and men and women were all equally naked. Some of the women carried their children on their backs, fastened by a rush cord. The men were all armed with pointed staves and with stones, which appeared to us to have cutting edges similar to iron axe-heads.

We noticed that these savages had generally small bilious eyes, full mouths, very white teeth, and flattened noses; their

---

[1] It was thought, until Bass's discovery in 1798, that Van Diemen's Land (Tasmania) formed part of New Holland (Australia).

hair, like that of the wool of Kaffirs, tied in peppercorn knots [*noués par pelotons*] and powdered with red ochre; the men had small natural parts and were not circumcized. Several amongst them had a sort of cicatrice on the skin on the chest. They appeared in general to be thin, fairly well made, with broad chests, and the shoulders well thrown back. Their language seemed to us very hard and they seemed to draw their voices from the bottom of the throat.

We endeavoured to gain their good will by means of presents, but they rejected with disdain all that we offered, even iron, looking-glasses, handkerchiefs, and pieces of cloth. They were shown fowls and ducks, brought from the vessel, in order to make them understand that we wished to buy the like from them. They took these animals, which by their action they showed to be unknown to them, and threw them angrily away. We had been examining these savages for about an hour when M. Marion landed. One savage stepped out of the group and offered him, the same as previously to the others, a firebrand, in order to light a little wood pile. The Commander, thinking that this was a ceremony intended to prove that he had come with pacific intentions, did not hesitate to light the pile, but it immediately appeared that this was all wrong, and that the acceptance of the brand was an acceptance of a defiance, or a declaration of war.

As soon as the pile was lighted, the savages retired precipitately on to a hillock, from which they threw a shower of stones, by which M. Marion, as well as an officer who was with him, was wounded. We immediately returned the fire and re-embarked. The gigs and longboats coasted along with the object of landing in the middle of the bay on a spot we had sighted where there was no neighbouring height from which those who landed could be molested. The savages then sent their women and children into the woods and followed the boats along the shore, and when we wished to land they opposed our doing so. One of them uttered a fearful cry, and the whole mob immediately threw their pointed sticks [spears] at us, by means of one of which a black servant was wounded in the leg; the wound was not serious, and the ease with which it was cured proved that these wooden javelins were not poisoned. As soon as they had thrown their javelins we answered by a fusilade, which wounded several, and killed one of them, whereupon they immediately fled into the woods, howling fearfully, and carrying with them those who, being wounded, could not follow them. Fifteen men armed with guns followed them up, and found at the outskirts of the forest one of the savages dying from the gunshot wound he had received. This man was five feet three inches high, and had his chest gashed like that of the Mozam-bique Kaffirs; he seemed black, but on washing him we found that his natural colour was reddish, and that it was only smoke and dirt that made him look so dark.

After the flight of the savages M. Marion sent two well-armed and officered detachments to look for fresh water and timber suitable for re-masting the *Castries*. The detachments scoured two leagues inland without meeting with either inhabi-tants, fresh water, or the timber.

We remained six days in Frederic Henry Bay, during which time we did not cease making vain search for fresh water. The land here is sandy like that at the Cape of Good Hope; it is covered with brushwood and small trees, from most of which the bark had been torn by the savages, who make use of it for cooking their shellfish. We found traces of fire every-where, and the ground seemed covered with ashes. In the midst of these trees despoiled of their bark and mostly burnt at the foot we noticed a sort of pine not so high as ours, which appeared well preserved, probably because the savages gained something useful from it, and therefore did not maltreat it as they did the others. It seemed to us that in going further away from the sea-coast and thus penetrating deeper inland, we should find these same pines in the valleys, but tall and thick enough for making into ships' masts.

In those parts from which the vegetation had not been burnt off, the soil was covered with grass and brake, similar to that in Europe, and also with sorrel. There was little game, and we presumed that the fires made by the savages in this place had driven them inland. Our hunters met a tiger cat, and found several holes like those in a warren; they killed some ravens similar to those in France, some blackbirds, thrushes, turtle doves, a parrokeet resembling a South American one in plumage with white beak. They killed all sorts of sea-birds, especially pelicans, and a black bird with red beak and feet, and which Abel Tasman mentions in his journal.

The climate of this southern portion of New Holland seemed very cold to us, although we were there in the middle of summer, and we could not understand how the natives could exist there in their naked state. What appeared more extraordinary to us was that we found no indication of houses, only some break-winds, rudely formed of branches of trees, with traces of fires near them. By the considerable heaps of shells which we met with from time to time, we judged that the ordinary nourishment of the savages consisted of mussels, pinna or wing shell, scallops, chama or heart cockles, and other similar shellfish.

We caught *chats-de-mer*, red fish like gurnets, cod, wrass, large quantities of very big rays, and many small fishes which were new to us. Our sailors caught many cray-fish, lobsters, and very big crabs; the oysters were very good and abundant. The collectors picked up star-fish, sea-urchins, scallops with long and spiny scales, *rouleaux*, *olives*, *cornets*, and several rare and very beautiful shells.

During our sojourn in this bay I made several longitudinal observations and found it to be situated in longitude 143° E. of Paris. I observed its latitude at 42° 50′ and took bearings.

It is remarkable that in coasting along Van Diemen's Land we met with very bad weather on the western coast, but on the eastern coast we found a clearer sky and more tractable winds.

DEPARTURE FROM NEW HOLLAND FOR NEW ZEALAND.

M. Marion, seeing that we were losing time in looking for water in a country as wild as its inhabitants, decided to set sail for New Zealand, where he hoped to find the water we were in want of, the necessary timbers for re-masting the *Castries* and the possibility of caulking the *Mascarin*, which was leaking badly.

On the 10th March [1772], we cleared Frederic Henry Bay and set sail for New Zealand, where we arrived on the 24th of the same month, without anything remarkable having occurred in the meanwhile.

New Zealand was discovered by Abel Tasman in 1642, but this Dutch navigator had in fact only discovered one particular spot. This portion of the southern lands has been visited lately by Captain Cook and M. de Surville. It is a strange coincidence that an English and a French vessel should have approached this country at the same time. M. de Surville had been in a bight, which he called Lauriston Bay, while the celebrated Captain Cook bore down on the two points which form the entrance to the very bay in which the Frenchmen were anchored and which he for his part called Double Bay. It is very surprising that Captain Cook did not learn from the savages of New Zealand, whose language he understood, of the arrival on these shores of a French transport, as he had moreover anchored once 20 leagues to the south and once 8 leagues to the north of the French vessel.

As soon as I obtained information of the voyage of the Englishman, I carefully compared the chart I had prepared of that part of the coast of New Zealand along which we had coasted with that prepared by Captain Cook and his officers. I found it of an exactitude and of a thoroughness of detail which astonished me beyond all powers of expression, and I doubt much whether the charts of our own French coasts are laid down with greater precision. I think therefore that I cannot do better than to lay down our track ·off New Zealand on the chart prepared by this celebrated English navigator. We landed at the foot of the high mountain named on this chart Mount Egmont. We named it *Mascarin Peak*, after our vessel. This peak is situated in latitude 39° 6' S. and 164½° E. of Paris. Captain Cook fixes this peak a few degrees more to the east.

We took this mountain for the cape which forms the Southern entry of Massacre Bay, to which Tasman gives an extent of

40 leagues.[1] We approached to within a league and a half of the shore, in order to reconnoitre, and saw some men and several fires. This mountain appeared to rise from the sea, and we judged it to be as high as the Peak of Teneriffe. The coast here is very steep, and we found a coral and stony bottom at 80 fathoms, about a league from land. M. Marion, fearing to be windbound here, stood off, and on 31st of March we returned to take bearings in latitude 36° 30'. From there we coasted along, sailing towards the north in quest of the Isles of the Three Kings.[2] The coast could be approached closely, there being deep water all along, and we sailed about one to three leagues off and found bottom at 26 to 40 fathoms.

While sailing along we were often attacked by squalls from the N. to the W. which obliged us to stand off. Finally on the 4th of April, at 9 o'clock in the morning, we perceived the islands, which from their position we judged to be those of the Three Kings. On the evening of the 5th of April, when we were close to these islands, we were again troubled with squalls, which obliged us to stand off. On the morning of the 13th we got to within a league of the islands and saw several men, who in the distance looked very tall. We noticed several groves of bushes which looked pleasant, but we were unable to discover the stream mentioned by Abel Tasman nor even a good landing place. All these islands may perhaps cover together an extent of about four leagues; the biggest was grassy and appeared inhabited; the others, six in number, were only barren and steep rocks.

Having made several vain attempts to land on the largest of these islands, we returned to the mainland about ten to twelve leagues off. On the 15th of April we made for land at the N.E. point of New Zealand, and to which Captain Cook in his

---

[1] Mount Egmont, in S. lat. 39° 18', and E. long. 174° 5', is on the east coast of North Island, whereas Massacre Bay, now generally known as Golden Bay, in S. lat. 40° 45', and E. long. 172° 45', is on the north coast of Middle Island. Marion's Expedition did not know of Cook's Straits or of the division of the country into islands.

[2] Discovered by Tasman in 1642 in S. lat. 32° 5', and E. long. 172° 0'.

charts gives the name of Cape *Maria Van Diemen*. We dropped anchor on the 16th in a cove situated in the most northern part of New Zealand, but where the ground did not hold well. We immediately sent a boat on shore in search of water at a spot where there appeared to be the mouth of a stream, but hardly had the boat reached the shore when a violent wind arose and the sea became very rough. The vessels dragged their anchors and we were both obliged to drop a second anchor. The boat had much difficulty in regaining the ship, and for fear of accident we had it hauled up at once. We then spent a very uncomfortable night. At daybreak the two ships were driving on to the land, so that we were obliged to set sail and abandon our cables and anchors. The wind was in the N.E., and should it have veered to the North, we should have had great difficulty in getting out of this cove.

After having tacked about to get clear of the shore, we returned to this same cove on the 26th and picked up our cables and anchors. On the 27th we got out again in search of a better anchorage. 1 noticed that along this shore there was a current of a league an hour, which during flood tide has an easterly course. On getting out we tacked to East and South. On 3rd May we sent a boat ashore to the east of a cape, which we called Cape *Quarré* on account of its shape, and which Captain Cook called Cape *Brett*.

When about two leagues off this cape we saw three canoes approaching us. There was little wind at the time and the sea was calm. One of the canoes, containing nine men, came close to the ship; so we made signs to the men to come on board, and sent them several nicknacks to encourage them. They came with some uneasiness and appeared not to be quite without fear when climbing the ship's side. M. Marion showed them into the chart room and gave them some bread, first of all he ate some, and then they followed suit. The liquor which was given them they drank with every sign of disgust. They were induced to take off their cloths, and instead of these shirts and trousers were given them, which they seemed to put on with pleasure. We showed them various implements such as axes, chisels, and adzes. They appeared very anxious to possess these, and made use of them at once in order to let us see that they understood their use ; these articles being given them, they went off shortly afterwards highly satisfied with their reception. As soon as they had got some distance away from the ship, we saw them take off their shirts and trousers in order to put on their former clothing, putting aside those we had given them. They then approached the other canoes, of which the occupants had not dared to accost us ; they seemed to reassure the latter (and to be inducing them to go and see us), who then came on board without showing the slightest signs of fear or distrust. There were two women amongst them ; we gave them some biscuits and some other nicknacks.

In the evening the wind having risen, the canoes returned ashore, but five or six of these savages remained on board of their own free-will. We gave them food and drink, they even supped with us, and ate with good appetite of all our dishes, but they declined to drink our wine or our liquor. They slept on board, we arranged beds for them in the saloon, and they slept well without showing the slightest distrust. They were, however, watched during the whole night. Amongst these savages their was one of their chiefs named *Tacouri*, of whom we shall have occasion to speak later on, and who showed great uneasiness every time the vessel turned from the shore in tacking about while waiting for the boat which had gone ashore in the morning.

The boat returned at eleven o'clock at night, and the officer in charge reported having found a bay round which there was a very considerable village which extended considerably inland, and where there appeared to be a good port, cultivated lands, fresh water, and wood. On the 4th of May, M. Marion sent two boats ashore, and we obtained the services of one of the savages to go with them and to point out to our people the places where they could water. The savage went willingly, and the boat started in quest of this cove. At 4 o'clock in the afternoon the boats returned with the water, and the officers reported having found good anchorage in this bay at 19 and 20 fathoms. They brought with them two other savages besides the one who had piloted them, and reported they had been received on shore by a large number of canoes, in which there were many men and women who were very friendly. That same day we anchored amongst the islands, and remained at anchor there until the 11th of the said month, when we sailed for a safer port which our boats had discovered on the 6th, but which, on account of contrary winds, we had been unable to get into sooner. Captain Cook has called this port the *Bay of Islands*.

SOJOURN ON THE NORTHERN PORTION OF NEW ZEALAND, CALLED EAKENOMAOUVÉ BY THE ABORIGINES.

DESCRIPTION OF THE COUNTRY AND NOTES ON ITS INHABITANTS.

On the 12th of May, 1772, the vessels being safely anchored, and the weather being fine, M. Marion erected tents on an island in the middle of the harbour, where there was wood and water, where there was a suitable cove opposite to the vessel, and whither he had the sick transported, and where he picketed a guard. The aborigines call this island *Motouara*.[1]

We had hardly anchored before a large number of canoes came off and brought us a quantity of fish, and which they explained they had caught expressly for us. At first we did not know how to talk to these savages, but by chance I bethought me of a vocabulary of the island of Taïty which had been given me by the superintendent of the Isle of France. I read several words of this list, and I saw with the greatest surprise that the savages understood me perfectly.[2] I soon saw that the language of this country was absolutely the same as that of the island of Taïty more than 600 leagues distant from New Zealand. On the approach of night the canoes retired,

---

[1] Dr. Thomson (Story of New Zealand, vol. i. p. 233) says the sick were landed on Te-Wai-iti, and not on Motu-Arohia, but he does not give his authority for the statement.

[2] It will be remembered Captain Cook made a similar discovery by means of a native of Taïty whom he had brought with him.

leaving on board eight or ten savages who remained the whole night with us just as though they were our comrades and had known us a long time.

Next morning being very fine many canoes came along filled with savages, who brought us their children and their daughters, all coming unarmed and with the greatest confidence. On arriving at the vessel, they commenced singing out *Taro*,[1] the name they give to ships' biscuit. We gave small pieces to every one, and that with the greatest economy, for they were such great eaters and so numerous that if we had given them according to their appetite, they would soon have consumed our provisions; they brought large quantities of fish, for which we gave them glass trinkets and pieces of iron in exchange. In these early days they were content with old nails two or three inches long, but later on they became more particular and in exchange for their fish demanded nails four or five inches in length. Their object in asking for these nails was to make small wood chisels of them. As soon as they had obtained a piece of iron, they took it to one of the sailors and by signs engaged him to sharpen it on the millstone; they always took care to reserve some fish wherewith to pay the sailor for his trouble. The ship was full of these savages, who appeared very gentle and even affectionate. Little by little they came to know the officers and called them by their names. We only allowed the chiefs, the women and the girls to enter the chart room. The chiefs were distinguished by the feathers of egrets or of other aquatic birds stuck in their hair on the top of their head. The married women were distinguished by a sort of straw plait which confined their hair on the top of the head; the girls had no such distinctive mark, their hair hanging naturally over their neck without anything to bind it.

It was the savages themselves who pointed out these distinctions and who gave us to understand by signs that we must not touch the married women, but that we might with perfect freedom make advances to the girls. It was in fact not possible to find any more approachable.

[1] Native edible root.

As soon as we discovered these distinctions, we passed the word round the two ships so that every one might be circumspect with regard to the married women, and thereby preserve the good understanding with savages who appeared so amiable, and not to cause them to be ill-affected towards us. The facility with which the girls were approached was the cause that we never had the slightest trouble with the savages on account of their women during the whole time we lived amongst these people.

I remarked with great astonishment that amongst the savages who boarded the vessels in the early days there were three kinds of men, of which those who appeared to be the true aborigines were yellowish-white and the biggest of them all, their mean height five foot nine to ten inches, and their hair black, glossy and straight; others were more swarthy and not quite so tall, their hair slightly frizzled [? curled]; finally there were true negroes with woolly heads, not so tall as the others but generally broader in the chest. The former have very little beard and the negroes have very much.[1]

The observations I made on these people during the following days on shore fully confirmed the correctness of my first remark. Generally speaking, these three kinds of men are handsome and well formed, with good heads, large eyes, well-proportioned aquiline noses and well-proportioned mouths, beautiful and very white teeth, muscular bodies, vigorous arms, strong hands, broad chests, extremely loud voices, small stomach, almost hairless well-proportioned but slightly gross legs, broad feet, and the toes well spread out.[2]

The women are not so good-looking on close examination; they have generally a bad figure, are short, very thick in the waist, with voluminous mammae, coarse thighs and legs, and are of a very amorous temperament, while on the contrary the men are very indifferent in this respect.

[1] These observations are very correct. There are two distinct races among the Maories, the black or Papuan, and the yellow or the Malayo-Polynesian.

[2] Darwin, who visited the Bay of Islands in December, 1835, makes a comparison between the appearances of the New Zealanders and the Taïtians very unfavourable to the former.

When we became well acquainted with the savages, they invited us to land and visit them in their village, the which we did. I disembarked with M. Marion, well armed and with a detachment of soldiers. We first of all wandered along a portion of the bay, where we counted 20 villages, composed of a number of houses, and large enough to lodge 400 people in every one. The smallest village would hold at least 200 inhabitants.

We entered several of the villages. From the moment we set foot on shore, the savages came unarmed to meet us with their women and children. We made friendly overtures to each other, and we offered them little gifts which seemed to please them much. The chiefs of some of these villages were most pressing with their invitations to go with them and we followed them.

DESCRIPTION OF THE VILLAGES OF THE NORTHERN PORTION OF NEW ZEALAND.

All the villages are situated on steep cliffs jutting out into the sea, and we noticed that where the inclination of the ground was not great, it had been made steep by hand. We had much difficulty in climbing up, and the savages had often to help us by holding our hands. On arrival at the top, we found first of all a palisade formed of piles, driven straight and deeply into the ground, seven or eight feet high, and the ground well beaten down and grassed at the foot of the palisades. Then followed a ditch about six feet broad, and about five to six feet deep, but this ditch was only placed on the land side, where an enemy might approach. There was then a second palisade, which, like the first, served to enclose the whole village into an oblong shape. The entrance gates are not placed opposite each other. After entering the first circuit one has to go further along a narrow path to look for the entrance through the second palisade. The gates are very small.

From that side from which they fear attacks they have a sort of outworks, equally well palisaded and surrounded by ditches, and which will hold four hundred to five hundred men. This work is only a palisaded oblong and is placed outside the village

FIG. 17.—Whole plant *Pteris aquilina*, showing creeping rhizome.

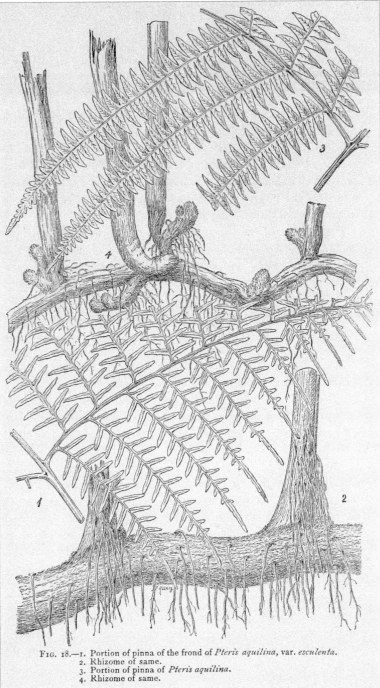

FIG. 18.—1. Portion of pinna of the frond of *Pteris aquilina*, var. *esculenta*.
2. Rhizome of same.
3. Portion of pinna of *Pteris aquilina*.
4. Rhizome of same.

to act as a defence to the entrance. Inside the village, at the side of the gate, there is a sort of timber platform, about 25 feet high, the posts being about 18 to 20 inches in diameter and sunk solidly in the ground. The people climb on to this sort of advance fort by means of a post with footsteps cut into it. A considerable collection of stones and short javelins is always kept up there, and when they fear an attack, they picket the sentinels there. The platforms are roomy enough to hold fifteen or twenty fighting men. These two outworks are generally placed at the outermost gate, and help to defend it as well as to prevent the ditch being crossed.

The interior of the village is composed of two rows of houses ranged side by side along the two sides of the palisades which form the enclosure, and every house is furnished with a pent-house, which serves as a kitchen. The savages eat their food under these sheds and never take a meal inside the house. The space which divides the two rows of houses, and which is more or less roomy, according to the lay of the ground, serves as a sort of parade ground, and extends the whole length of the village. This parade ground is raised about a foot higher than the surrounding ground on which the houses stand. It is raised by means of soil brought there and beaten down; no grass is to be seen on it and the whole place is kept extremely clean. This whole space between the two rows of houses is only occupied by three public buildings, of which the first and nearest to the village gate is the general magazine of arms. A little distance off is the food storehouse, and still further the storehouse for nets, all the implements used in fishing, as well as all the necessary material for making the nets, etc. At about the extremity of the village there are some large posts set up in the form of gallows, where the provisions are dried before being placed in the stores.

In the centre of this parade ground there is a piece of wooden sculpture representing a hideous figure very badly carved, on which one can only recognize a rude head, eyes, a great mouth, very much like the jaws of a toad and out of which protrudes an immoderately long tongue. All the other portions of the

body are still more shapeless, with the exception of the genital parts, occasionally of one sex, occasionally of the other, which are represented in greater detail. This piece of carving is part of a huge pile sunk deeply into the ground.

We entered with the chiefs into the first magazine where the arms are stored; we found a surprisingly large quantity of small wooden spears, some simply with sharpened points, others carved in the form of serpents' tongues, and these carvings continued for the length of a foot from the tip of the javelin, others furnished with very sharp points made from the bones of the whale. We also found bludgeons or clubs made of some very hard wood and of ribs of the whale which are still harder; spears which seemed made on the model of our ancient halberds for spearing at one end and clubbing at the other, these lances being all of a very hard wood and fairly well carved; tomahawks of stone or of bones of whale, the tomahawks being highly polished, well sharpened and neatly carved; sticks furnished at one extremity with knotted cord for throwing darts in the same way as we throw stones with slings; and some varieties of battle-axes in hard wood and fairly well designed for killing people.

In this same magazine we found a collection of their common implements, such as axes, adzes, chisels made of various very hard stones such as jade, granite, and basalt. The magazines are generally about 20 to 25 feet long by 10 to 12 broad. In the interior there is a row of posts which support the ridgeboard of the roof. The savages arranged their arms round these posts like a stand of arms according to variety.

In the second magazine, where the savages keep their food in common, we found sacks of potatoes, bundles of suspended fern-root, various testaceous fishes, cooked, drawn from the shell and threaded on blades of rushes and hung up; a large quantity of fragments of big fish of every variety, cooked, wrapped up in packets in fern leaf and hung up, and an abundance of very large calabashes always kept full of water for village use. This storehouse is almost as big and of the same shape as the magazine house.

3

The third storehouse contains the rope, fishing lines, the flax for making rope, thread and rushes for making string, an immense quantity of fishhooks of every size from the smallest to the largest, stones cut to serve as lead weights, and pieces of wood cut to serve as floats. In this warehouse they keep all the paddles of their war canoes; it is there that they make their nets, and when they have finished one they carry it to the extremity of the village, or every net in the form of a seine to a separate cabin.

These public storehouses as well as the private houses are made of timber, well squared and fastened by mortise and tenon and pinned together; they are generally oblong in form; instead of planks for the walls of their houses, they make use of well-made straw matting, which they ply doubled or trebled one on top of the other, and which shelter them from wind and rain. The straw mattings also serve as roofs to the houses, but in this case they are made of a sort of very hard grass which grows in the marshes, and which the natives manipulate with great skill. Every house has only one door about three feet high and two feet broad, which they close from the inside by means of a latch very much like the iron one which we use in France for closing our gates. Above the door there is a small window about two feet square furnished with a rush trellis; inside the house there is no flooring, but they take the precaution to raise the soil about a foot and beat it down well so as to avoid damp. In every house there is a square of boards well joined together about six feet long and two feet broad; on these planks are laid seven or eight inches of grass or fern leaves well dried, and upon which they sleep. They have no other beds. In the middle of the house there is always a small fire to drive out the dampness. These houses are very small, being for the most part not more than seven or eight feet long by five or six feet broad. The houses of the chiefs are larger; they are ornamented with pieces of carved wood, and the posts in the interior are also carved. The only furniture we found in these houses were fishhooks of mother-of-pearl and of wood and bone, nets, fishing lines, some calabashes full of water, stone implements such as we had seen in the common store-houses, mantles and other clothing hanging on the partition.

The whole of the villages which we saw during our two months' stay in the Bay of Islands appeared to be constructed on the same plan without any well-defined differences. The construction and form of the private houses as well as those of the chiefs were the same in all the villages; they were all palisaded and placed on high cliffs. At the extremity of every village and on the point which jutted furthest into the sea there was a public place of accommodation for all the inhabitants.

The Food of the Inhabitants of the North of New Zealand.

We were extremely well received by the savages. They came in mobs on to the vessels and appeared there every day, and we went similarly to their villages and into their houses with the greatest security. This naturally gave us every facility for seeing how these people fed themselves, what were their occupations, their works, their industry, and even their amusements.

We have already noticed that the basis of the food of these people is the root of a fern absolutely similar to ours, with the sole difference that in some places the New Zealand fern has a much bigger and longer root and its fronds grow to greater length.[1]

Having pulled up the root they dry it for several days in the air and sun. When they wish to eat it they hold it before the fire, roast it lightly, pound it between two stones, and when in this state they chew it in order to obtain the juices, which to me appeared farinaceous; when they have nothing else to eat, they eat even the woody fibre; but when they have fish or shellfish or some other dish, they only chew the root and reject the fibre.

These people live also principally on fish and on shellfish;

---

[1] The New Zealand fern is *Pteris aquilina*, var. *esculenta*, and the European species is *Pteris aquilina*. The difference is thus very slight. See Figs. 17 and 18.

they eat quail, ducks and other aquatic birds which abound in their country, also various species of birds, dogs, rats, and finally they eat their enemies.

The New Zealanders have no vessel in which to cook their

meat; the general custom in all the villages we visited was to cook the meat and fish in a sort of subterranean oven. In every kitchen there is a hole one and a half feet deep and two feet in diameter; on the bottom of the hole they place stones, on the stones they place wood which they light, on this wood they place a layer of flat stones which they make red hot, and on these latter stones they place the meat or fish which they desire to cook.

They also live on potatoes and gourds, which they cook in the same way as their meat. Their habits in eating are dirty.

I have also seen them eat a sort of green gum which they like immensely, but I was not able to find out the tree from which they obtained it. Some of us ate of this by letting it drop in our mouths. We all found it very heating.

We also remarked that the savages eat regularly twice a day, once in the

FIG. 5.   morning, the other time at sunset. As they are all strong, hardy, big, well-formed, and with good constitution, one concludes that their food is very healthy, and I think it well to repeat here that fern root forms the basis of their food.

Generally speaking they appeared to me to be great eaters; when they came on board our vessel, we could not satisfy them sufficiently with the biscuit which they liked immensely. When the sailors were eating they would approach them in order to get a portion of their soup and of their salt meat. The sailors used to give them the remains on their platters, which the savages took care to clean out thoroughly; they were very fond of fat and even of tallow. I have even seen them take the tallow from the sounding lead or tallow otherwise used in the ship and eat it as a tasty morsel.

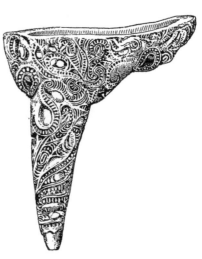

FIG. 6.

They were very partial to sugar; they drank tea and coffee with us, and liked our drinks according as they were more or less sweetened. They showed great repugnance for wine, and especially for strong liquors; they do not like salt and do not eat it. They drink a great deal of water, and when I saw them very thirsty, I used to think that this desire to be continually drinking was caused by their dry food, the fern root.

The Clothing of the Savages of the North of New Zealand.

The savages in this part of the world never wear any head-dress; they tie their hair into a tuft on the top of their heads with a piece of cord or plaits of grass, and then cut it off in the form of a round brush an inch or two above the cord; for want of scissors for this operation they make use of a shell the edges of which they sharpen. The men and women rub fish oil into their hair and powder it with crushed red ochre. Many of them only powder the tuft, and the chiefs adorn their heads with white plumes.

The married women arrange their hair the same as the men; the girls allow their hair to fall naturally on their necks, and cut it so that it does not grow below the shoulders.

Young women paint their lips black, which is no doubt done in order the better to show off the whiteness of their teeth.

The ears of the men are pierced like those of the women, and they all equally adorn them with mother-of-pearl and lustrous shells, or with feathers, or with small dogbones.

Some wear round their necks pieces of jade of a very fine green of various forms joined together, engraved or carved. Some of this jade glitters very much. They sometimes wear mother-of-pearl, pieces of wood, or bundles of feathers.

The women wear necklaces made like rosaries, composed of broken pieces of equal lengths of white teeth alternately with black irregular tubes; others wear necklaces made of small very hard black stones of a fruit which I do not know.

Men and women wear a mantle on their shoulders, held up by means of a plait round the neck, and which hangs down as far as the waist. These mantles are made of a small piece of coarse stuff, without seam, and made for this purpose only: they just exactly cover the shoulders and the back, and leave the chest and stomach uncovered.

Besides this mantle, they have a sort of cloth of the same material, which envelopes the waist and thighs, and hangs as far as the calf of the leg. This second garment is, like the first, common to both men and women; it is bound and held round the waist by a belt about four fingers wide. These belts are sometimes made of the same material, and sometimes of plaited rushes.

They have invented another sort of garment which is in fact a waterproof mantle. This mantle is made of very coarse flax, of which the fairly long ends stick out above the tissue; the side of the material thus bristling with long strings, like skin with the hair on, the savages put on the outside to receive the rain, which thus runs off as from a roof. The mantle is long, and covers almost the whole body.

The chiefs are distinguished from the rest of the people by

mantles and loincloths of finer tissue. I noticed that only
the chiefs had very nicely worked mantles, with very
fine thongs of dogskin
adroitly twisted close together, with the colours
arranged symmetrically,
and having the appear-
ance of consisting of a
single skin. They put
the hair inside touching
their skin when it is cold,
and outside when it is

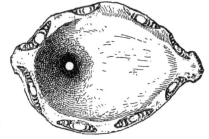

Fig. 7.

warm. But the most striking way discovered by the chiefs
of these savages to distinguish themselves has been to
engrave (tatu) their face and buttocks in the most hideous
manner: they draw designs by means of small pricks on the
forehead, cheeks, and even the nose, and as the blood runs out
they rub powdered charcoal into the outer skins, and which
cannot be effaced. They study to invent designs which make
them look horrible and give them a most fearful look. All these
designs on the faces of the various chiefs are very varied, but
the designs on the buttocks are always the same: on these
parts they trace in equally indelible marks a very neat spiral
line, of which the first point is on the centre of the most fleshy
part, and successively embraces the whole circumference.

They have also on both hands two little black engravings
drawn very correctly in the form of an " S." The chiefs
were very pleased to show us all the tatuings on their bodies,
and seemed even proud and conceited about them.

THE ARTS OF THE SAVAGES IN THE NORTH OF NEW ZEALAND.

The arts of these savage people are almost confined to four
objects: to procure sufficient nourishment, a simple lodging
against the inclemencies of the climate, the garments necessary
in a climate colder than appears consistent with the position of
their islands, and finally, to fortify themselves and to insure them-

selves against invasions by their fellows, and even to attack and destroy the latter.

I have already mentioned that the fern root is the basis of their food. This root naturally grows very deep in the soil, and in order to dig it up they have invented a sort of pointed spade very much like a lever pointed at one end, to which they have fixed transversely a piece of wood, strongly bound with cord, which serves as footpiece, while they work the lever at the other end with their arms, to send it deeply into the ground, and are thus enabled to raise large clods. As this lever has only a certain breadth at the end which is pushed into the ground, two men join together to work it to lift the same clod. This sort of spade very much resembles a stilt on which the step is placed at about two and a half feet from the bottom.

These people have already made a start in the art of agriculture. They cultivate a few small fields of potatoes similar to those of the

Two Indies, they also cultivate gourds, which they eat when they are small and tender, and when they are ripe they take out the inside, dry them, and make use of them for carrying and conserving water. Some of their calabashes will hold as much as from ten to twelve pints of water.

They also cultivate an aloes-pite and a sort of *reed*,[1] which, when ripe, furnishes them, after retting, with thread to make their cloth, and cords for various uses. In the cultivation of these crops they make use of the same instrument of which I have just spoken, sharpened and trimmed so as to form a sort of spade. It seemed to me that they confined their whole agriculture to two or three objects. They have no knowledge of any sort of grain and, excepting some small fields planted with potatoes, gourds, aloes-pite, and very small flax, the whole country appeared to me to be lying fallow, and producing only the wild natural growths. I

FIG. 8.

[1] By this is here probably meant the New Zealand flax.

saw nothing which might be taken for an orchard, and I did not even meet with the least fruit, either wild or cultivated.

As fish, after the fern root, forms their staple food, their arts are particularly directed towards all that concerns fishery. Without iron, or any other metal, they make hooks of all sizes out of mother-of-pearl and various other shells, all worked with great skill. Their fishing lines, as well as their nets of every description, are knotted with the same adroitness as those of the cleverest fisherman of our seaports; they manufacture seines five hundred feet long; and for want of corks to hold up the net, they make use

FIG. 9.

of a very light white wood, and for lead to weigh it down, they make use of very heavy round pebbles enclosed in a net-work sheath which runs along the bottom of the seine.

They manufacture their seines of reeds and a sort of well-twisted thread, coloured red with fish oil. The knots of these seines are exactly similar to those of our nets.

All the villages situated in the middle of the Bay of Islands, where we anchored, possessed a considerable number of canoes. These boats, which were dug-outs, appeared to be generally well made, with lines calculated for speed, well worked, and more or less carved. The majority of the canoes were 20 to 25 feet long by two and a half to three feet broad. Their principal use is for fishing, and every canoe ordinarily carries seven or eight men.

Besides these boats, which appeared to be private property, every village possesses in common two or three big war canoes for attacking purposes. I measured one of them which was seventy feet long by six feet broad and four deep, made of the body of a single tree trunk, the two sides of which were raised by means of planks skilfully sewn on, the sewing well caulked, and the whole canoe painted red by the aid of oil. These war canoes have carved, and very high, poops and prows.

The savages make use of paddles instead of oars; these

paddles are of most perfect cut, and so shaped as to add by
the elasticity of the blade to the force of the stroke. In certain
points these paddles might serve as models to the boatmen of
our ports. The paddles of the chiefs, who ordinarily command
the canoes, are nicely carved on the back.

What is astonishing in the arts of the savages, in the construction of their boats, of their paddles, in their carvings, in
fact in all their works, is that they have no iron nor any other
metal which can take its place; as a consequence they have
none of the tools which our workmen make use of. In lieu
thereof they have very hard stones sharpened and formed like
iron axes, chisels, and adzes. The stones they chiefly use for
this purpose are jade and basalt. It is no doubt a great art to be
able to substitute for iron materials so raw and so varied. However, this art is common to all savages known in different parts
of the globe, and the tools of the Australians are exactly the
same as those which have been found in New Guinea, in New
Holland, amongst the islanders of the South Seas, and finally
amongst the inhabitants of America when that part of the
world was first discovered.[1] It is even probable that before the
discovery of iron and of the method of smelting it, so as to
adapt it to our uses, the primitive inhabitants of the earth, the forefathers of all those nations of to-day who have made the greatest
advances in the arts, commenced by making use of stone tools.
It is probable that they made use of these rude tools for a
long time and perhaps for centuries.

The boats of New Zealand are all built of a splendid
cedar with which the country abounds. By following M. du
Hamel's[2] method for obtaining the specific weights of wood, I
found that the New Zealand cedar when freshly cut did not

[1] When these words were written, travellers were not in the habit of making
minute examination of the weapons, etc., of savages. While all savages make
use of stone in some shape or other for their implements and weapons, there
is a vast difference between the palaeolithic form almost as found in nature as
made use of by the Tasmanian and the neolithic highly finished article produced
by the New Zealander.

[2] Professor at the School of Mines, Paris, b. 1730, d. 1816.

weigh above a pound and a half more per cubic foot than the best quality of Riga pine.

I have already mentioned that the savages feed on shellfish. The procuring of this sort of nourishment does not call forth any special art, and the women and girls go daily to collect it off the rocks in the sea. For this purpose they put on a rush apron made like matting to save their petticoats from the sea-water; round their waists they carry a rush basket, into which they collect the shellfish and carry it to their villages. These savages know of no other method of capturing game than the net and the running noose; with these they catch quail, wild ducks, a very large species of wood pigeon, and several other kinds of birds of which I shall speak later on. They do not know the use of the bow and arrow.

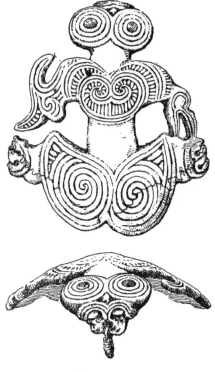

FIGS. 10, 11.

I have already spoken of the arts of the Austral savages in the formation and arrangement of their villages, in the construction of their public storehouses and of their private dwellings. The arts employed in the manufacture of their garments cover a large number of objects. They cultivate flax and know how to ret it. After retting they beat it in order to detach the hard or woody portion, they then comb their thread with combs made of large sea-shells, and lastly they have a sort of crude and simple wheel and distaff for spinning their thread. They make also a thread of five or six strands of hair which is very strong. Finally they have a method of working which seems to be the commencement of that followed by our weavers, and by which they make cloth of very close tissue and of good wear.

It would be impossible to estimate the immeasurable distance there exists between the rude industries of the savages and those which amongst enlightened nations serve their wants and their luxuries. It is impossible to imagine the trouble and the enormous loss of time savages suffer from the imperfection of their arts; one must perhaps have seen the insufficiency and the fatiguing efforts of these industries of early man, emerging as it were from the hands of nature, in order to be sensible how grateful we ought to feel towards those who by their labours from century to century have so perfected all our arts.

The savages of New Zealand live in a continual state of warfare; their palisaded villages, surrounded by ditches and situated on very high cliffs, prove that they fear their enemies and are always on the defensive. This continual state of warfare has inclined their labour towards the manufacture of every species of implement useful for destroying their fellows, and has brought about the use of stone, wood, and bones of animals to that end. Their tomahawks are of stone, generally of basalt, and sometimes of jade. Their lances, their javelins, and their pikes are made of a very hard and heavy wood; their clubs or bludgeons are made of wood and of the bones of whales; their war trumpets are of wood and give out a very disagreeable sound similar to that of shepherds' horns. All these murderous instruments are carved and worked with care, and the savages possess large quantities of them.

Nevertheless all their arms are ridiculous and contemptible when opposed to men armed in European fashion: fifty fusiliers with sufficient ammunition, and who might have to revenge themselves on these people, could without danger destroy them like wild beasts and entirely exterminate them.

Besides these destructive instruments they have two or three varieties of flutes from which they extract fairly sweet but at the same time discordant sounds by breathing into them with their nostrils. I have heard them play on these instruments, especially in the evening when they were locked up in their villages, and it appeared to me they sometimes dance to the sound of the flutes.

The Religion of the Savages of the Northern Part of New Zealand.

We did not remain long enough in New Zealand, and I was always too much occupied with the wants of our vessels, to be able to acquire satisfactory notions regarding the worship and belief of the savages. I have, however, sufficient grounds for believing that they have some religion, and these are as follow :

1. They have in their language a word which expresses the Divinity; they call it *Ea-Toue*, a name which describes one who makes the earth tremble.

2. When they were asked questions on this subject, they raised their eyes and hands towards heaven with demonstrations of respect and fear, which indicated their belief in a Supreme Being.

3. I have already said that in the middle of every village there is a carved figure which appears to represent the tutelary god of the village. In their private houses are to be found similar figures like little idols placed in positions of honour. Several savages carried similar figures carved in jade or in wood round their necks. These figures are simply hideous, they nearly all have an immoderately long tongue and have a fearful look, and if these images represent their divinity, they prove that the people regard him as an evil being. It is possible that in their opinion all these figures only represent the demon authors of evil which differ from the Divinity.

4. I noticed that the savages who came to sleep on board our vessels were in the habit of communing with themselves in the middle of the night, to sit up and mumble a few words which resembled a prayer in which they answered one another and appeared to chant. This sort of prayer generally lasted eight or ten minutes.

5. If there were any savages on board our vessels when we went to prayers, they did not appear astonished; they took up the attitude of the sailors, and appeared to join in their prayers.

CONTINUATION OF OBSERVATIONS AND OF VARIOUS EVENTS WHICH TOOK PLACE DURING OUR STAY IN THE BAY OF ISLANDS IN NEW ZEALAND.

A few days after our arrival in the Bay of Islands M. Marion made several journeys along the coast, and even into the interior of the country, in search of suitable timber for making masts for the *Castries*, and in these excursions the savages accompanied him everywhere. On the 23rd of May M. Marion discovered a forest of magnificent cedars about two leagues inland, and within reach of a bay about a league and a half distant from our vessels.

We immediately made a settlement there. We sent thither two-thirds of our crews with axes, tools, and all the necessary apparatus, not only for cutting down the trees and making masts thereof, but also to smooth a road over three small hills and across a marsh, which had to be traversed in order to bring the masts to the sea-shore.[1]

We established barracks in communication with the settlement on the shore nearest to the place where we had our workshop; to this post our vessels sent daily boats laden with provisions for the workmen who were hutted two leagues inland.

We had three posts on land. One was on the island *Moutouara* in the middle of the bay, where we had our sick under tents, our forge where we made the iron bands for the re-masting of the *Castries*, and also our empty casks, with the coopers, for it was on that island that we obtained our water. This post was guarded by an officer, with ten armed men, and the surgeons at the service of the sick. A second post was on the sea-shore

---

[1] Dr. Thomson writing in 1859, eighty-seven years after the event, says: "Part of the cut down tree and the road made to drag it along still remain, and was pointed out to me as the road of Marion" (Story of New Zealand, vol. i. p. 235).

of the mainland, a league and a half from our vessels, which
served as store and as point of communication with our carpenters'
workshop situated two leagues further off, in the middle of the
forest. These two latter posts were equally under the command
of officers, who had armed men under them in order to guard
our goods.

The savages were always amongst us at our settlements and
on board our vessels, and in exchange for nails they furnished
us with fish, quail, wood-pigeons, and wild duck; they ate with
our sailors and helped them in their labours; and every time
they set to work, the result was very noticeable, for they were
extremely strong, and their help relieved our crews very
much.

Our young men, attracted by the winning ways of the savages,
and by the friendliness of their daughters, overran the villages
every day, even making journeys inland to hunt the ducks, and
taking with them the savages, who carried them across marshes
and rivers as easily as a man would carry a child.

It sometimes happened that they strayed very far so as to
get among savages of another canton, and to find there villages
very much bigger than those in our bay. There they found
men with whiter skins, who received them very well, and they
occasionally returned in the middle of the night through the
forests, accompanied by a mob of savages, who carried them
when they were fatigued.

In spite of these proofs of friendship on the part of the savages,
we were always a little on our guard, and our boats never went
ashore without being well armed; neither did we allow the savages
to come on board our vessels when they were armed. But at last
confidence was established to that pitch that M. Marion gave
orders that the whale boats and gigs going ashore should be
disarmed. I did all that I possibly could to get this order re-
scinded, and in spite of the winning ways of the savages, I never
forgot that our predecessor, Abel Tasman, had named Massacre
Bay that bay where he had land-fallen in New Zealand. We did
not know that Capt. Cook had visited it since, and had made
an entire survey; neither did we then know that he had found

the people cannibals, and that he was to be killed in the same bay in which we were now anchored.[1]

It is very surprising that savages, who in the preceding year had seen and traded with a French and an English vessel,[2] and who must necessarily have obtained from these ships iron, cloth, and other European goods, should never have allowed us to notice anything about this, and should never have given us to understand that they had seen other vessels besides our own. It is true that the goods we gave them daily were never seen again by us, nor did we see any traces of them in overrunning their villages and on visiting their houses.

Lulled into a feeling of the greatest security, it was M. Marion's greatest happiness to live in the very midst of these savages. When he was on board, the council chamber was full of them; he fondled them and with the help of the Taïty vocabulary he tried to make himself understood. He overwhelmed them with presents. They on their part recognized perfectly that M. Marion was the chief of the two vessels; they knew that he liked turbot, and every day they brought him some very fine ones. Whenever he showed a desire for anything, he always found them at his orders. Whenever he went ashore, all the savages accompanied him as though it were a day of feasting, and with joyful demonstrations; the women, the girls, and even the children petted him. They all called him by name.

So great was the confidence established that *Tacouri*, the previously-mentioned chief of the largest village, brought his son on board to M. Marion, aged about fourteen years, whom he

FIGS. 12, 13.

[1] Cook was killed in the Hawaiian Islands, and not in this bay.
[2] De Surville's and Cook's vessels are those referred to here.

appeared to love very much, and whom he even allowed to pass the night in the ship.

When three of M. Marion's slaves deserted in a canoe, which sank on reaching the shore, *Tacouri* had those who had not been drowned arrested, and sent them back to M. Marion.

One day a savage entered by the port hole of the powder-magazine and stole a sword; he was discovered, made to come on deck, and was denounced to the chief, who severely repri-manded him, and who begged that he should be put in irons just like a sailor. The thief was however sent away without punishment.[1]

We had become so familiar with these men that nearly all the officers had particular friends amongst them, who served them and accompanied them everywhere; had we departed about this time, we would have brought to Europe the most favourable accounts of these savages; we would have painted them in our relations with them as the most affable, the most humane, and the most hospitable people on the face of the earth. From our accounts philosophers fond of praising primitive man would have triumphed in seeing the speculations of their studies confirmed by the accounts of travellers whom they would have recommended as worthy of belief. But we would all of us have been in the wrong.

On the 8th of June M. Marion had landed, accompanied by a mob of savages as usual. He was received with greater demonstrations of friendship than ever; the chiefs assembled and by common accord appointed him Grand Chief of the country, and they stuck in his hair on the top of his head the four white plumes which serve to distinguish chiefs. He returned on board more pleased with the savages than ever.

While this was going on the young savage for whom I had grown to have a great affection, who came to see me every day and who showed great attachment towards me, paid me a visit; he was a fine young man, well made, with a sweet expression and always smiling. On this particular day he appeared sorrowful in a way in which I had never seen him before. He brought

---

[1] See remarks of l'Abbé Rochon in the Introduction.

me as a present some arms, implements, and ornaments of a
very beautiful jade which I had expressed a desire to possess.
I wished to pay him for these things with iron implements and
red handkerchiefs, which I knew would please him, but he
refused them. I wished to make him take back his jade, but
he would not. I offered him something to eat, he refused again
and went away very sorrowfully. I never saw him afterwards.

Some other savages, friends of our officers and accustomed
to come and visit them every day, disappeared at this time, but
we did not pay sufficient attention to the fact. We had been
thirty-three days in the Bay of Islands and lived on the very
best of terms with the savages, who appeared to us to be the best
people one could possibly meet with; we spread into the country
every day in order to reconnoitre, to study its productions and see
if we could discover any metals or other objects fit for commerce.
M. Marion had sometimes gone very far in his gig, and had
visited various bays inhabited by other savages, all of whom had
received him well.

On the 12th June at two o'clock in the afternoon, M. Marion
landed in his gig armed with a dozen men, taking with him
two young officers MM. de Vaudricourt and Le Houx, and a
volunteer and master-at-arms, altogether sixteen people. The
above-named *Tacouri*, the chief of the largest village, another
chief, and five or six savages who were on board, accompanied
M. Marion, whose object was to go and eat oysters and run the
seine at the foot of the chief's village.

At nightfall M. Marion did not return to sleep at his usual
hour. No one returned from the gig, but none of us were
alarmed, as the hospitality of these savages was so well known
to us that we did not distrust them in the least. We merely
thought that M. Marion and his followers were remaining to
sleep on land in our huts in order to be nearer in the morning
to the workshops, two leagues inland, where the masts of the
Castries were being made. The masts were approaching com-
pletion, and part of the materials had already been transported
close to the shore, the savages helping us every day with these
fatiguing transports.

The next morning, the 13th June, the *Castries* sent the longboat ashore for wood and water for the day's consumption, it being customary for the two vessels to send alternately every day for common wants. At nine o'clock, however, a man was seen swimming towards the vessels, and a boat was immediately lowered to help him and bring him on board. This man was one of the longboat's crew, who alone had saved himself from the massacre of his comrades— murdered by the savages. He had two spear- wounds in his side and had been badly hurt. He stated that when the longboat landed at seven o'clock in the morning, the savages had appeared on the shore without arms and with their usual demonstrations of friendship, that they had even as was customary carried such sailors who were afraid to wet their feet on their shoulders from the boat to the shore, that they had shown themselves as good fellows as hitherto, but that when the sailors had separated one from another in order to pick up their bundles of wood, the savages attacked them furiously, in bands of eight or ten for every sailor, with tomahawks, clubs, and spears, and so murdered them. As for himself, as he had only to do with two or three savages, he at first defended himself and received two spear-wounds, but seeing other savages approach, he had run off and hidden himself in the brushwood. From there he had seen his comrades killed, and how that the savages having killed them, stripped them, cut open their stomachs, and commenced hacking them to pieces. He then started to reach the vessel by swimming.

After such a fearful account we doubted no longer that M. Marion and the sixteen men in

Figs 14, 15.

the gig, of whom we had no news, had suffered the same fate as the eleven men of the longboat.

The officers who still remained on board immediately met together in order to consult about saving the three stations we had on land.

The *Mascarin's* longboat, well armed with an officer and a detachment of soldiers commanded by a sergeant, was immediately despatched ashore. The officer had instructions to search the length of the coast for the gig of M. Marion and for the longboat, but he was above all instructed to warn the stations and to go first to the landing place nearest to the mastyard in order to carry the greatest help to this station with the news of what had happened. The officer discovered the longboat of the *Castries* and M. Marion's gig stranded together at the foot of *Tacouri's* village and surrounded by savages armed with axes, swords, and muskets which they had taken from the two boats after having slaughtered our people.

In order not to lose any time, the officer did not stop at this place, where he might easily have scattered the savages and retaken the boats, for he feared lest he might be too late to arrive in time at the mastyard station, and he stuck to his orders to carry prompt help thither with news of the tragic events of the morning and of the day before.

Fortunately I was at the station, having passed the night there. I had not slept, but without knowing anything of the massacre of M. Marion, I had kept a good watch. I was on a little hill and occupied in directing the transport of our masts, when about two o'clock in the afternoon I saw a detachment marching towards us in good order with bayonets fixed, which I recognized at a distance, on account of their brightness, as not being the ordinary arms of the ship.

I understood at once that this detachment had come to give us news of something wrong. In order not to frighten our men, as soon as the sergeant, who was at the head, was within hailing distance, I ordered him to stop, and I alone approached so as to ascertain what was the matter. As soon as I heard his report, I ordered the detachment to preserve silence and marched with them to the station.

I immediately stopped all work and had the implements and arms collected, the muskets charged, and divided amongst the sailors all that they could carry away. I had a hole dug in one of the barracks in order to bury the rest. I then had the hut pulled down and burnt, so that the few implements and utensils which I had buried, as not being able to carry away with me, might be hidden under the ashes.

Our men knew nothing of the misfortunes which had overtaken M. Marion and their comrades, for it was necessary that they should not lose their heads if we were to get out of the trouble. We were surrounded by armed savages whom I had only then perceived when the detachment joined us and after the sergeant had made his report. The assembled savages occupied the surrounding heights.

Fig. 16.

The detachment, now reinforced by the sailors armed with muskets, I divided into two divisions; one division headed by the sergeant led the way, the sailors carrying the implements and other effects following in the centre, and I followed in the rear with the other half. We were about sixty men. We passed several mobs of savages, of whom the various chiefs repeated frequently the sad words, "*Tacouri maté Marion*," that is to say, "The chief Tacouri has killed Marion." It was the intention of the chiefs to frighten us, for we had learned that amongst them when a chief is killed in a quarrel, all is lost for his followers.

We thus marched two leagues to the sea-shore, where the long-boats awaited us, without having been harassed by the savages, who contented themselves with following alongside and frequently repeating that Marion was dead and eaten. There were in the detachment several good marksmen, who, hearing that M. Marion was killed, were burning to avenge his death and frequently asked my permission to break the heads of those chiefs who appeared to threaten us. This was, however, not the time to occupy ourselves with vengeance. In the state in which we were then, the death of a single man would have been an irreparable loss, and had we lost several, the two vessels might never have left New Zealand. We had besides a third station, that of the sick, which had still to be placed in safety. I accordingly restrained the ardour of our men, and prohibited them from firing, promising to give their vengeance full play at a more favourable opportunity.

When we arrived at our longboat, the savages began to press us more closely. I ordered the burdened sailors to embark first, then addressing one of the savage chiefs, I fixed a peg in the ground ten paces from him, and gave him to understand that if a single savage crossed the line of the peg I should shoot him with my carbine, which I raised in apparent readiness for action. I told them in threatening tones to sit down. The chief repeated my order quietly to his people, and immediately the savages, about a thousand strong, sat down.

I made all our people embark, which took long enough, because there was much baggage to put in the longboat, and the boat when loaded could not be launched easily, and we were obliged to wade into the water in order to start her. I was the last to embark, and as soon as I had entered the water, the savages rose *en masse*, crossed the marked line, and uttering their war cry, threw wooden spears and stones at us, which did harm to nobody. They burned our huts on the bank, and threatened us with their arms, which they beat together, uttering fearful yells. As soon as I got into the boat, I had the grapnel raised and so arranged the men that they should not interfere with the oarsmen. The boat was so over-loaded that I was obliged to stand up in the stern with the arm of the rudder between my legs. I did not intend to fire a single shot, but intended to re-join the vessel promptly in order to send the longboat to *Moutouaro* Island, and there relieve the invalid station, our forge and cooperage.

As we began to get away from the shore the cries and threats of the savages increased to such an extent that our departure looked like a retreat, and the savages entered the water as though determined to attack us. Much to my regret I found it advisable and necessary for our safety that I should make these unhappy people understand the superiority of our arms. I had the rowing stopped, and ordered four fusiliers to fire at the chiefs, who appeared more excited and animated than all the others. Every shot told, and this fusilade continued some minutes. The savages saw their chiefs and comrades fall in the most senseless manner, they could not understand how they could be killed by arms which did not touch them like their tomahawks and clubs.[1] At every shot they re-doubled their cries and threats; they were most horribly excited, and as they remained on the shore like a flock of sheep, we might indeed have killed every man of them had I desired to continue the firing; but after having killed many more than I wished to, we rowed on to the vessel, while the savages did not leave off shouting.

As soon as I arrived on board the *Mascarin*, I despatched the longboat to relieve the sick station. I sent a detachment commanded by an officer with orders to send on board all the sick, the surgeon's assistants, and all the utensils of our hospital,

---

[1] This statement sounds strange when we remember that for more than a month the natives had opportunities of seeing wild fowl killed with guns.

to pull down the tents, to make an entrenchment with our casks round the forge for the night, to picket an advance sentinel on the side towards the village which was on the same island, to keep a good watch and to take every precaution against a surprise, for I feared some attack by the savages on our forging establishment, where the iron would very likely tempt them. At the same time I arranged with the officer in charge for signals during the night, and promised to send him prompt assistance in case of attack.

The sick were happily brought on board without accident towards eleven o'clock at night. The savages prowled round about the post, but seeing our people well on guard, they dared not make an attack, having failed to surprise them.

The next morning, the 14th June, I sent a second detachment with a couple of officers on to the island. We had not as yet sufficient wood and water on board to enable us to continue our voyage, and after our experience with the savages, we should have had much difficulty in raising these stores on the mainland.

The island *Moutouaro*, placed as it was in the middle of the harbour close to our vessels, gave us as much wood as we wanted and there was a fresh water spring for filling our casks; but as there was on this island a village of about three hundred savages, who might be in a position to trouble us, I instructed the officer in charge of the station that in case the aborigines were disposed to be troublesome, he should unite all his forces, attack the village, and clear the whole island of them, so as to insure our water supply.

In the afternoon the savages appeared armed close to the station, and made threatening demonstrations as though defying our men to fight them. Our men immediately prepared to receive them, marched upon them with bayonets fixed, but without firing; for the savages fled into their village, where they made a firm stand, uttering fearful yells.

Malou, the chief of the village, who was one of those with whom we had lived most familiarly, was accompanied by five or six other chiefs or principal fighting men from other villages; they were intensely excited, and incited, by their voices and the movement of their arms, the young fighting men to advance upon us, but these dared not.

Our men in battle array arrived within pistol shot of the gate of the village; there they commenced firing, killing six chiefs, whereupon the whole of the fighting men fled across the village in order to get to their canoes. The detachment pursued them with the bayonet, killed about fifty, overthrew some of the others in the water, and set fire to the village. By this means we became masters of the island. We merely had one man severely wounded by a spear which struck him in the upper part of the nose in the corner of the eye.

After this expedition we re-embarked our forge, our iron, and our casks, and I had the whole station withdrawn. I then had the ferns on the island cut down, for fear the savages might hide in them and surprise us, for they grew six feet high and very thick. I had the dead savages buried, leaving one hand sticking up out of the ground in order to let the savages see that we did not eat our enemies. I had recommended our officers to make an effort to bring us some savages alive, and to try and catch some young people of both sexes or children; I had even promised the soldiers and sailors 50 piastres for every living savage they might bring me; but the islanders had taken the precaution before the battle to place their women and children in safety by carrying them over to the mainland. Our soldiers attempted to stop and bind such of the wounded as could not flee, but these wretches were furious and bit like wild beasts, others broke the cords with which they were bound just as though they were thread, so that it was not possible for us to secure even one.

In the meanwhile the *Castries* was still wanting bowsprit and mizenmast, and it was quite out of the question to go and fetch the beautiful cedar (Kauri pine) masts which we had found on the mainland, and which had cost us so much infinite trouble to get out of the forest where we had cut them down. We therefore rigged up some jury-masts as best we could.

We still wanted seven hundred barrels of water and seventy cords of firewood for the two vessels, and as we only had one longboat for this work, we completed it bit by bit in the course of a month, sending the longboat to the island every day to get wood and water alternately. The workers were always accompanied by a detachment which returned on board every night.

One day when the longboat remained longer than usual, the savages crossed over to the island in large numbers on that side where they could not be seen. The sentinel posted on a piece of rising ground saw a man with a hat and dressed like a sailor approaching him; but this man walked like one who sneaks along and does not wish to be observed. The sentinel called out to him to stop, but it was a savage, who, not understanding him, continued to advance. The sentinel recognized the disguise, fired and shot the man. Immediately a multitude of savages were seen to approach; the detachment advanced, chased them, and several which were killed were found dressed in the clothes of the officers and sailors they had previously murdered; the rest of the savages re-embarked in their canoes, and after this useless attempt they did not again molest us.

From the day on which M. Marion disappeared, we could see from the vessels every movement of the savages who had retired to the mountain strongholds; we could clearly distinguish their sentinels posted on the highest parts, and from whence they notified to their friends the least of our proceedings. Their eyes were always turned towards us, and we could distinctly hear the calls of the sentinels who answered one another with a most surprisingly powerful voice. During the night they signalled by means of fires.

When the savages appeared in mobs within gunshot of our artillery, we now and then fired a cannon ball at them, especially during the night, in order to let them know that we were on the alert; but as they always kept out of cannon shot they never experienced the effect, and it was to be feared that they would become so emboldened as to despise our artillery.

One of the canoes, in which there were eight or ten men, passed one day within gunshot of the *Castries*, which cut the canoe in two by means of a cannon ball and killed some of the savages, the others regaining the land by swimming.

In the meanwhile we were not sure of the fate of M. Marion, of the two officers who accompanied him ashore on the 12th of June, nor of the fourteen sailors he had taken with him in his gig, partly to row and partly to draw the seine. We only knew, from the account of the sailor who had escaped the massacre of the boatmen the following day, that the eleven men killed in this horrible treachery had had their stomachs cut open after being killed, and their bodies quartered and distributed amongst the savages who had massacred them. The sailor who had been fortunate enough to escape had observed this horrible scene through the brushwood, where he had concealed himself.

In order to throw some light on the fate of M. Marion, and on that of his companions in misfortune, I sent the longboat with trustworthy officers and a strong detachment to the village of *Tacouri*, who the savages told us had killed M. Marion, where we knew he had been fishing, accompanied by this same *Tacouri*, and where we had seen his gig, as well as the longboat, stranded and surrounded by armed savages. I instructed the officers to make the most minute search, first of all in the place where we had seen the stranded boats, and then to enter the village, to force it if it was defended, to exterminate the inhabitants, to rummage scrupulously through all their public buildings and private houses, to pick up whatever they could find having belonged to M. Marion or to his companions in misfortune, so as to be able to confirm their death by an official report, to wind up by setting fire to the village, and by carrying off the big war canoes which were hauled up at the foot of the village thereof, or by burning them in case they could not tow them away.

The longboat left well armed with swivel guns and blunderbusses, and landed first of all at the place where we had seen our stranded boats. These were no more, the savages having burned them in order to extract the iron. The detachment then marched in good order on to *Tacouri's* village. Traitors are cowards in New Zealand the same as elsewhere: *Tacouri* had fled: he was seen afar off out of gunshot range, having on his shoulders M. Marion's mantle, which was made of English cloth of two colours, scarlet and blue. His village was abandoned, and only a few old men remained who had not been able to follow their fugitive comrades, and who were seen sitting quietly in front of their houses. Our men wished to take them captive. One of them without appearing to get excited struck one of our soldiers with a javelin which he had by him. Our men killed him, but no harm was done to the others, who were left in the village. The men rummaged all the houses carefully. They found in *Tacouri's* kitchen the skull of a man who had only been cooked a few days before, some pieces of flesh were still hanging on to it, and on these we could trace the marks of the cannibal's teeth. They also found a piece of a human thigh fixed to a wooden skewer and three-parts eaten.

In another house they found the body of a shirt which was recognized as having belonged to M. Marion. The neck of the shirt was all bloody and there were three or four blood-bespattered holes in the side. In other houses they found part of the clothes and the pistols of young M. de Vaudricourt, who had accompanied M. Marion on the fatal fishing excursion; finally were found the arms of the longboat and a heap of rags from the clothes of our unfortunate sailors.

After having made a thorough visitation of the village and having collected all the proofs of the assassination of M. Marion and of his companions, and also the arms and articles abandoned by the savages, fire was set to the houses and the whole village reduced to ashes. While this was going on the detachment noticed that the islanders were leaving a neighbouring village very much better fortified than the others, belonging to a chief named *Piquioré*, who was the accomplice of *Tacouri*. The detachment immediately marched on to this village but found it completely deserted. The houses were visited, and as in the former village, several articles from our boats and shreds of clothing from our massacred people were found. Among others in *Piquioré's* kitchen they found human entrails, recognized as such by one of our surgeons, cleaned and cooked. This village was also reduced to ashes.

On their return our people launched two war canoes and towed them to the vessel. We took out planks and wood, which might prove useful; but as we could not take the body on board, which was about sixty feet long, it was burned.

As soon as we had confirmed the death of M. Marion, we searched in his papers for any of his plans for the continuation of the voyage, but we only found some very detailed notes in the form of instructions from the Governor of the Isle of France, which, leaving M. Marion to his own operations and researches, merely indicated the best method of making the observations, of directing them towards objects which might prove most useful to our colonies, and generally towards the advancement of human knowledge.

The two ships' staffs having been assembled, we found that we had lost our best sailors, that the *Castries* had but three anchors, three cables, and her longboat; that the masts of this vessel, being formed of a collection of small material, could not have the same strength as if they had been made of suitable timber; that we had many sick on board; and finally that we had provisions for eight or nine months only, even supposing that all we had was in good preservation.

It was in consequence decided by common consent that we should proceed with our journey in the South Seas according to M. Marion's intentions; but that, without searching for distant lands, we should confine ourselves to reconnoitering the islands of Rotterdam and Amsterdam, where we might procure fresh provisions, that from thence we should sail for the Iles la Borne, or Marianne Islands, in order to get to the Philippines, where we might get a cargo and thence return to the Isle of France.

This plan being decided upon, we completed our stores of wood and water; we took possession in the King's name of the Island of New Zealand, which the Aborigines called *Eakénomaouvé*, and which M. Marion had called *France Australe*; and we prepared to leave the bay to which M. Marion had given his name, for he had discovered it in his gig. Captain Cook had called it on his chart the Bay of Islands, and we named it on leaving *Treachery Bay*. It is situated in S. latitude 35° 10′ and 174° longitude to the E. of the meridian of Paris. The magnetic variation is 12° N.E.

Before leaving New Zealand I shall give an account of my general observations on the manners of its inhabitants, of which I have already given some details in the course of this narrative. I shall then speak of that which I was able to observe regarding the physical aspect of the country and of the different products of its soil.

General Observations on the Manners and Customs of the Inhabitants of the Northern Portion of New Zealand.

After what had happened to us, and the investigations we had made, we could not doubt that the savages of this part of New Zealand were cannibals. Mr. Cook, the English Captain, who had visited them shortly before us, learned from them themselves that they only ate their enemies, and our sailor who had escaped from the longboat had been the sorrowful witness of the cruelty with which these aborigines divided amongst themselves the bodies of those whom they had killed. It is to be presumed that they regarded as enemies all strangers, even those of their own island who lived at a distance from their village. This barbarous custom seems to me common to all savages who are found scattered in the different corners of the earth; but when I remember the interesting demonstrations of friendship which these Australasians had manifested towards us, unaltered for thirty-three consecutive days, in order to butcher us on the thirty-fourth, I cannot believe that there can be on the face of the earth greater traitors than these savages. I can affirm that not even on the slightest occasion had these savages any reason to complain of us. The friendship which they showed us was carried to the extremest familiarity; the chiefs on boarding our vessels entered our rooms without ceremony, and slept on our beds, examining all our furniture piece by piece; they asked about the meanings of our pictures, and of our mirrors, of which they of course understood nothing. Indeed, they spent whole days with us with the greatest demonstrations of friendship and of confidence. Two days before murdering him they had of their free will proclaimed M. Marion Grand Chief, and on the day on which they had decided to murder him and his companions, in order to feast on them afterwards, they brought him some very fine turbots as a present.

Here then we have a picture of these primitive men, so extolled by those who do not know them, and who attribute gratuitously to them more virtues and less vices than possessed by men whom they are pleased to call artificial, because forsooth education has perfected their reason. For my part I maintain that there is amongst all the animals of the creation none more ferocious and dangerous for human beings than the primitive and savage man, and I had much rather meet a lion or a tiger, because I should then know what to do, than one of these men. I speak according to my experience. Having been occupied with the art of navigation ever since my childhood, I have never been able to enjoy that happy ease which permits of those studies and contemplations by means of which philosophers improve their minds; but I have traversed the greater part of the globe, and I have seen everywhere that when reason is not assisted and perfectioned by good laws, or by a good education, it becomes the prey of force or of treachery, equally as much so among primitive men as amongst animals, and I conclude that reason without culture is but a brutal instinct.

During the whole time that we lived in a sort of confidence with these primitive men I had endeavoured to study their characters, and I succeeded in doing so as much as was possible considering the difficulties we had in understanding each other through an imperfect vocabulary, of which several words were different to those in their dialect. I had made myself familiar with several chiefs and with young and old men, and they had easily become so towards me. Every day I probed their inclinations and inquired into the capacity of the lights of their reason; I understood that they only had a faint idea of a Supreme Being and of some subsidiary invisible creatures, that they were somewhat afraid of these latter and prayed frequently to them, that the object of these prayers was to become the conquerors and butchers of their enemies, that every family considered itself independent and stranger to the others, that they had no other law, no other police, and almost no other instinct, but that which was necessary for self-preservation. They were more contented when we gave them sugar, bread or meat than when we made them presents of useful articles such as axes, chisels or other implements.

At times I endeavoured to arouse their curiosity. I even sometimes imitated them in order to discover the workings of their souls, but I only found wicked children, and all the more dangerous, for being as they were stronger and even hardier than the generality of men. Within the space of a quarter of an hour, I have seen them pass from the most silly joy to the darkest sorrow, from calmness to fury, and return as suddenly to immoderate laughter. I have seen them turn and turn about, sweetly affectionate, hard and threatening, never long in the same temper, but always dangerous and treacherous.

In accordance with the results of such observations repeated day after day for thirty-three days, I always mistrusted them and always noted with the acutest sorrow how M. Marion took these savages into his confidence, a confidence to which at last he fell a victim in spite of my most serious representations.

One can easily conceive how it is, that amongst a people like that of New Zealand, which are in a state of continual warfare, separated by little doubly palisaded villages surrounded by ditches, and built on almost inaccessible heights, the fighting man holds the first place. We did not notice amongst them any distinction save for the purposes of war. Those only met with consideration who best knew how to use a tomahawk or to handle the club or lance.

Only those amongst the fighting men who have committed acts of ferocity or treason have the right to wear four plumes in their hair, to tatu the skin of their face, their buttocks, and their hands, and which is considered amongst them as the

highest distinction. There is no doubt that in order to arrive at the pre-eminence of such complete tatuing a man must have killed and eaten many of his fellows.

When an ordinary man, woman, or child dies, the corpse is thrown intó the sea; but a fighting man is buried, and on the hillock which covers his corpse spears and javelins are stuck as trophies.

A country inhabited by a people which only respect the art of destroying their fellows, cannot be thickly populated, and so it appeared to me that the interior of the country was uninhabited, and that a population was only to be found on the coast along the harbours. At our first anchorage we found a large village abandoned and destroyed, and although I sometimes climbed high mountains, in order to get a view of the country, I could only find dwellings on the sea-coast. A people which frequently fight, and amongst whom the conqueror eats the conquered, are the most destructive people that can possibly exist. Nevertheless these ferocious men love dancing, and their dancing is of the most lascivious character; they frequently danced on the deck of our vessels, and they danced so heavily that we were afraid they would break through the deck. In dancing they sing alternately warlike and lascivious songs.

The two sexes do not know shame, and although they are half clothed against the cold, they go about quite naked without ceremony when they no longer fear it.

The men show great indifference towards the women, and make them do all the domestic and laborious work. The women collect in the fields the bundles of fern root pulled up by the men; they carry water from the foot of the mountains up to the villages; they alone collect the mussels and other shell-fish on the sea-shore; they alone do the cooking, prepare the dishes and serve them to the men without eating with them; they are in fact in that state of degradation which makes them the servants rather than the companions of their husbands.

The women in general are not so well made as the men, and no doubt it is the laborious works to which they are sub-jected which makes them thick and misshapen. Nevertheless I

5

did see some young women who were pretty. They seemed to be good mothers and showed affection for their offspring. I have often seen them play with the children, caress them, chew the fern root, pick out the stringy parts, and then take it out of their mouth in order to put it into that of their nurslings.

The men were also very fond of and kind to their children. The chief *Tacouri* sometimes brought his son on board; he was about fourteen years of age with a pretty face, and the father seemed to love him very much.

When their relations die, they mourn for them several days. Mourning consists in scratching the face and all parts of the body to express sorrow, in assembling in the house of the defunct to weep and utter cries of despair, in recounting his deeds and howling at the end of every account.

On the whole I did not see many children. One has to associate with them for a long time before one can become acquainted with their manners, laws and customs. At sight of these big, hardy and well-made men, one suspects that they do not preserve those children who are born sickly or deformed.

I noticed that the men and women attain to a great age, that they preserve up to the most advanced age all their hair, which does not whiten much, and their teeth are more used up than spoilt. We did not find any traces showing them to be subject to small-pox or venereal diseases; they are generally slovenly and wash but little, but neither pock mark nor cicatrice is to be seen on their skins. There were, however, amongst our crews several sailors who suffered from the usual diseases, which they communicated to the people of the country.

It is no doubt surprising that we should have found at this corner of the earth, in islands unknown until the present day, and cut off from all communication with other parts of the globe, three varieties of man: whites, blacks, and yellows. It is most certain that the whites are the aborigines. Their colour is generally speaking like that of the people of Southern Europe, and I saw several who had red hair.[1] Amongst them there were some

---

[1] In these cases the red colour of the hair is probably produced by washing in wood ashes, etc.

who were as white as our sailors, and we often saw on our ships a tall young man five feet eleven inches high, who by his colour and features might easily have passed for an European. I saw a girl, fifteen or sixteen years of age, as white as our French women. Various occurrences in navigation might have transferred the blacks of New Holland to New Zealand, which are about 300 leagues distant, but which may not always have been so far off. New Holland, the largest island we know of, has certainly been peopled by the blacks of New Guinea, from which it is only separated by a strait as broad as a river. These negroes transported to New Zealand have no doubt allied themselves with the women of the country, and from these alliances have no doubt sprung the yellow people we see at the present day.

It is to be observed that, in almost all the islands which extend from Formosa and the Philippines as far as New Zealand in this great Archipelago, which occupies an area of more than fifteen hundred leagues in length between the seas of China, the Indies and Africa, on one side, and those of America on the other, we find everywhere a prodigious mixture of men of different colour and cast, whites, especially negroes and the yellows. The shores of Formosa are inhabited by Chinese, the interior of the island by half-savage blacks; the shores of Luzon and the majority of the other Philippine Islands are inhabited by Malay colonies, and their interiors, the forests and the mountains, by true wild aborigines. The same holds good of Borneo, where woolly-headed negroes are found; the same with regard to the Malaccas, New Guinea, Timor, New Holland, and finally New Zealand. Perhaps we shall find the same mixture in the Austral lands which the French and English are this day vying with each other in their attempts to discover. What is most singular is that our navigators have quite recently found the same mixtures even as far as the middle of the South Sea in the island of Taïty.

Perhaps there was a time when New Zealand communicated with the island of Taïty, from which it is at present separated by a sea with no bottom and more than six hundred leagues in extent. At New Zealand we found the same language as that of Taïty, with a few differences in a small number of words, and there is much resemblance between these two peoples so widely separated at the present day.

I am not disinclined to believe that America was peopled by New Zealand, the Austral lands and the islands of the South Sea. I find a striking resemblance amongst the manners and customs of savages of these different parts of the globe: the same men almost beardless and cannibals, the same arms, the same utensils, the same cut of clothes, habitations, and boats; the same indifference towards the women, the same manner of making them do all the most laborious work. Those who have a good knowledge of the languages of these people will perhaps find greater analogy. The chapter which follows may perhaps give additional evidence in favour of the conjecture.[1]

PHYSICAL OBSERVATIONS ON NEW ZEALAND AND ON SOME OF ITS NATURAL PRODUCTIONS.

Seamen are generally not sufficiently well educated to be able to report, in the accounts of their voyages, on the sometimes very interesting objects they meet with in the countries they overrun, especially on unknown regions and peoples which they discover for the first time. To be able to journey usefully one should have a knowledge of all our arts and a smattering at least of natural history, and a little of that philosophy so necessary for studying without prejudice the mind and the opinions of primitive man, the varieties and the immensity of the works of creation, and the slow revolutions and even the agitations of nature in different portions of our planet.

When Captain Cook, who on his corvette has just completed one of the most interesting voyages ever made since the time of Magellan, and who, by an astonishing succession of discoveries and by incredible labour, has merited from his country and the human race generally the position of being ranked amongst the most celebrated navigators, was sent by England to the

---

[1] These paragraphs must be accepted for what they are worth, and do not coincide with our present knowledge of human migrations.

South Seas, three scientific men, Messrs. Banks, Solander, and Green, were given him as companions. These three learned men, associated with the great seaman, have drawn from this splendid but laborious voyage all that it was possible to do for the advancement of human knowledge.

When we were despatched from the Isle of France in October, 1771, for the journey of which I am now giving an account, M. l'Abbé Rochon, of the Academy of Sciences, as well as M. Commerson,[1] a learned naturalist, were to have started with us. The former had already rendered important services to navigation by determining the position of several islands and reefs situated between the Isles of France and Bourbon and the Coromandel and Malabar coasts; he had also, conjointly with an officer of great distinction, M. le Chevalier de Fromelin, ship's captain, his relation and friend, just saved the vessel *Le Berrier* from missing the Isle of France by correcting the ship's reckonings, by means of very precise longitudinal observations, which reckonings had an error of more than a hundred leagues, ascribed solely to the currents. The latter had collected an immense quantity of plants during M. de Bougainville's voyage round the world. M. Poivre, the Governor of the Isle of France, had engaged these two scientific men to accompany us; but fortunately for them this clever and virtuous administrator, who was ceaselessly occupied with all that which might contribute to the progress of science and to the advantage of navigation, was not able to overcome the obstacles which ultimately prevented their departure—obstacles which consisted in another mission which was considered more important. M. Marion and I were all the more grieved at this as we were about to open up an absolutely new route for entering into the South Seas, and an astronomer furnished with good instruments and with an excellent chronometer by the celebrated Ferdinand Berthoud,[2] would have made our voyage infinitely more useful.

---

[1] Philibert Commerson, a French botanist, who died at the Isle of France, 1773. There is a curious story relating to his botanical valet, who followed him round the world, and who was discovered by the natives of Taïty to be a woman.

[2] The chronometer maker, born in Neuchatel 1725, died at Paris 1807.

After the partial survey I had made of the productions of New Holland, and especially of those of New Zealand, I often had cause to regret that these two learned men had not been able to embark with us. I feel perfectly sure I have not been able to see as with their eyes; but encouraged by the hope of indulgence towards a traveller, who after all is only a seaman, I will relate ingenuously and in good faith that which has struck me most.

Having been accustomed during a long succession of voyages in all parts of the world to read in the great book of Nature, and to note above all her most striking scenes, I first of all observed that the mass of the land of New Zealand looked like a great range of mountains, which might formerly have formed a portion of some great continent　The various highest peaks of this range were for the most part covered with snow. On its western shore there is not the slightest appearance of a plain—it is rocky; the land is much broken, without coves, havens or ports, and appears but little inhabited. From the sea we could not sight any estuaries.

The eastern coast, which faces the South Sea, is more cut up with a multitude of islands, bays and harbours, and it seems that all the rivers coming from the mountains have their course and run into the sea on this side. One sees plains which look delicious and appear to be well wooded.

In overrunning this part one finds everywhere volcanic traces, lava mixed with scoriæ, basalt or compact lava, pumice stone, blocks of that black glass which is known only to be the result of volcanic fusion [obsidian], baked earths in a friable form like tripoli, and others less friable and more mixed. Might not the subterranean fire, which formerly burned and vitrified so much matter in New Zealand, have also by several shocks detached this island from New Holland or from the Austral lands or from some other continent? According to South Sea travellers all the lands, which extend from New Zealand from south latitude 47° to the equator, and from the equator to the north of Japan, and from thence to the 40° north latitude, are after all only islands, so that this vast portion of our globe, which extends North and South for eighteen hundred leagues, resembles a ruin. We find everywhere traces of extinct or active volcanoes close to one another. This immense space which bounds our entire planet to the east and to the south appears to be the abode of fire: it seems that there Nature has placed her formidable workshops, and her efforts for ages past have changed and during our days still change the face of this part of the earth, make it tremble without ceasing, break it up by depressions and terrible explosions, and make it totter under the feet of the unfortunate inhabitants. It is not without good cause that the islanders of Taïty and the savages of New Zealand agree in calling the Divinity the "One who shakes the earth." People so widely separated and without a knowledge of the art of navigation do not speak the same language unless they were once the same people and inhabited perhaps the same continent, of which the volcanic shocks have only spared us the mountains and their savage inhabitants, and who by means of their former easy intercommunication are now mixed black and white. In this great portion of the earth so long unknown to Europe and so little known at this day, how many physical revolutions may not have been occasioned by successive volcanic eruptions? How many cities, empires, nations, may have disappeared from the face of the earth and abandoned their abode to the element which now covers them, like the city of Callao, which was covered and engulphed by the sea on the night of the 28th October, 1747? We are assured that on the coast of Peru some years ago a fairly considerable rock was discovered which is composed of an immense mass of petrified human bones, as though the sea had formerly covered a vast cemetery, of which the corpses petrified under the waters appear to-day in the form of a rock. This fact supports my conjecture regarding the existence of submerged countries between New Zealand and Taïty, etc. I shall not be astonished if those navigators, now occupied with the discovery of an Austral Continent, should find at the Antarctic Pole nothing but islands, being the summits of the mountains which have escaped from volcanic shocks and have been separated from plains which may formerly have surrounded them. There they will surely find people absolutely similar to those of New Zealand.

In my wanderings on the land which surrounds the Bay of Islands I found here and there blocks of white marble, of red jasper, ideous marble which suggests that there exists in this island some marine deposit around the nucleus of the ancient rock of granite, the base of which appears to be gabbro laminated and more or less black, containing a white substance which is pulverulent and dull in some, but brilliant and solid in others; crystallized quartz, firestone, flint, chalcedonic agates, pebbles crystallized in the interior, others translucent and similar to those which one finds in India on the Malabar coast. In the first bay in which we anchored, and where we lost our anchors, I found a spring of very soft water running out of the rock, and whose waters appeared to me to be capable of producing petrifaction. I picked up the remains of a petrified crab, some pebbles of which the kernel was very hard, and of which the outer layers folded like leaves had not yet acquired the same hardness, although of a strong nature.[1] I found masses of flints formed into very large blocks, being bound together by a hard natural cement.[2] Finally we found everywhere a very beautiful red ochre indicating the ferruginous nature of the soil.

Although it appears that jade is very common in New Zealand, for the savages have nearly all tomahawks, chisels, engraved images, and ear ornaments made thereof, yet I was not able to see the place where they obtain it; I do not know whether they find it in the rivers like pebbles or whether Nature has placed it in quarries.[3] This jade is of a beautiful semi-transparent green, and of a deeper hue than that of the jade known to other parts of the world; sparkling pieces are sometimes found which are of a very pleasing variant colour. The New Zealanders carve all their implements with jade, which is one of the hardest stones.[4]

---

[1] Probably concretions with concentric coats shelling off the outside.

[2] A siliceous conglomerate perhaps like the well-known Hertfordshire Pudding-stone.

[3] It is found in old rocks, probably metamorphic, on the west coast of South Island.

[4] There are plenty of works on the geology of particular districts of New Zealand. Hochstetter's Physical Geography, Geology, and Natural History is very good, but out of date. There is a capital sketch of the Geology of the

The country which surrounds the Bay of Islands is a charming mixture of plains and slopes, valleys and mountains. Wherever the country is not covered with forest, it is covered with ferns; those which grow on the sea-coast and on the mountains are not much higher than those of France, but those which grow in the dales and at the foot of the mountains are the large ferns which the savages prefer on account of their roots, which are as thick as one's thumb, and which form the basis of their nourishment.

Their forests contain a fairly large variety of trees, amongst which I recognized a very beautiful strong-smelling myrtle thirty to forty feet high, *Guaiacum* [sic] *atherosperma*, and several red-wood trees, one of which resembles the small-leaved *bois de natte à petites feuilles* [mysine] of the Isles of France and Bourbon. We obtained from this good knees for repairing our vessels. But the tree which prevails most in all the forests is the olive-leaved cedar [*Dammara australis*, the Kauri pine]. I have had cedars of this variety cut down whose trunks were more than a hundred feet long, from the ground to the lowest branches, and fifty-two inches in diameter. The trees are very resinous: the resin is white and transparent, and gives out an agreeable smell like incense when burnt. It appeared to me that this cedar is the commonest and highest tree of the country; its wood is elastic, and I judged it very suitable for making ships' masts.[1]

Islands in the Handbook of New Zealand, by Sir James Hector, but it is short; the section on Economic Minerals is fuller. But a better sketch, entitled Outline of the Geology of New Zealand, appeared in the Detailed Catalogue and Guide to the Geological Exhibits (New Zealand Court, Colonial and Indian Exhibition, 1886) by Sir James Hector. It contains a good coloured geological map, and is regarded as the most convenient work of reference on the subject.

[1] ". . . the famous Kauri pine. I measured one of these noble trees, and found it thirty-one feet in circumference above the roots. There was another close by, which I did not see, thirty-three feet; and I heard of one no less than forty feet. These trees are remarkable for their smooth cylindrical boles, which run up to a height of sixty and even ninety feet, with a nearly equal diameter, and without a single branch. The crown of branches at the summit is out of all proportion small to the trunk; and the leaves are likewise small compared with the branches. The forest was here almost composed of the Kauri; and the largest trees, from the parallelism of their sides, stood up like gigantic columns of wood" (Darwin's Voyage, 24th Dec. 1835).

In some parts the forests are very free from obstructions, in others the ground is covered with shrubbery, some of which is thorny, and with a very common vine which climbs to the top of the very highest trees.

Although we were in New Zealand in the months of June and July, which months are the coldest in this southern portion of the world, I did not see a single tree shed its leaves. The forests were quite as green as they are in France in the middle of summer; nevertheless there were occasional light frosts, and in the morning I have seen the water of the marshes frozen over to a thickness of two or three lines, but the sun melted this thin ice within an hour of its rising. I did not see any snow fall in the plains, but I have noticed it on the highest mountains. I also noticed that the rains generally came from the E. and N.E., which is contrary to the direction they come from in our French climate.

The marshes are full of rushes and of *Hibertia* (?). On stony ground, on slopes which are not broken up, we found a variety of *Hoheria* in large quantities, from which these savages extract a very beautiful silken thread, a cyprus-leaved tithymale [sic] resembling a shrub, different sorts of *Epacris, Solanum, Aviculare,* and a very pretty golden immortelle. In the neighbourhood of the sea we found very tasty celery, also *Oxalis magellanica,* a kind of large leaved water-cress,[1] and the same variety of *morel* which is eaten in Madagascar and in the Isle of France. We ate a good deal of these plants, which abound in the country, and the eating of which had a very salutary effect on our scurvied people when the good terms on which we lived with the savages allowed us to gather them every day. The savages expressed great astonishment at seeing us eat these herbs.[2]

I formed a garden on *Moutouaro* Island, in which I sowed the seed of all sorts of vegetables, stones and the pips of our fruits,

---

[1] Water-cress, *Nasturtium officinale,* is believed to have been introduced long after this date.

[2] For information regarding vegetable food of New Zealanders, see Colenso on the Vegetable Food of the Ancient New Zealanders in Transactions New Zealand Institute, vol. xiii.

wheat, millet, maize, and in fact every variety of grain which I had brought from the Cape of Good Hope; everything succeeded admirably, several of the grains sprouted and appeared above ground, and the wheat especially grew with surprising vigour.

The soil is excellent for vegetation.[1] In those parts where I was obliged to stir the ground, in making the road for transporting our masts, I found it to consist of a black vegetable soil down to a depth of five to six feet, without any other admixture. At this depth the soil was mixed with small stones and more especially with small translucent pebbles.

The garden on *Moutouaro* Island alone was not sufficient to satisfy my desires; I planted stones and pips wherever I went —in the plains, in the glens, on the slopes, and even on the mountains; I also sowed everywhere a few of the different varieties of grain, and most of the officers did the same. We tried in vain to get the savages to grow some, and explained to them the use of the wheat, of the other elementary grains and of the quality of the fruits of which we showed them the stones. But they had no more mind for this than brutes.[2]

---

[1] "New Zealand is favoured by one great natural advantage : namely, that the inhabitants can never perish from famine. The whole country abounds with fern; and the roots of this plant, if not very palatable, yet contain much nutriment. A native can always subsist on these, and on the shell-fish, which are abundant on all parts of the sea-coast. . . . The whole scene, in spite of its green colour, had rather a desolate aspect. The sight of so much fern impresses the mind with an idea of sterility : this, however, is not correct ; for wherever the fern grows thick and breast high, the land by tillage becomes productive " (Darwin's Voyage, 23rd Dec. 1835).

[2] "At one place we found a number of people collected round an object which seemed to attract general attention, and which they told us, when we entered the circle, was tabooed. It proved to be a plant of the common English pea, and had been growing about two months. The seed that produced it had been found in the *Coromandel*; it was fenced round with little sticks, and the greatest care appeared to be taken of it " (R. A. Cruise, Journal, p. 211).

"The excellent plants left by Captain Cook, viz. cabbages, turnips, parsnips, carrots, etc., etc., are still numerous, but very much degenerated ; and a great part of the country is overrun with cowitch, which the natives gave Marion the credit of having left among them " (*Ibid.* p. 315).

"In many places I noticed several sorts of weeds, which, like the rats, I was forced to own as countrymen. A leek has overrun whole districts, and will prove

In several places I found very good potters' clay, and our master gunner, a very ingenious man, rigged up a potter's reel, on which in the presence of the savages he made several vessels, porringers and plates, and even baked them under the very eyes of the savages. Some of his essays succeeded perfectly, and he gave the articles to the savages who had seen them turned and baked, but I doubt whether they will profit by such an industry as this, which would afford them a thousand conveniences.

The only quadrupeds I saw in this country were dogs and rats. The dogs are a sort of domesticated fox, quite black or white, very low on the legs, straight ears, thick tail, long body, full jaws but more pointed than that of the fox, and uttering the same cry; they do not bark like our dogs. These animals are only fed on fish, and it appears that the savages only raise them for food. Some were taken on board our vessels, but it was impossible to domesticate them like our dogs, they were always treacherous and bit us frequently. They would have been dangerous to keep where poultry was raised or had to be protected; they would destroy them just like true foxes. The rats are of the same species as those we have in our fields and forests.[1]

We had on board our vessels some pigs from the Cape of Good Hope, some sheep and kids, the sight of which caused the greatest astonishment to the savages every time they came on board. They looked upon these animals with the greatest surprise, proving that they have not the like in their country. They had also never seen domestic fowls and ducks, and were very much astonished to see them in the coops. They have absolutely no other domestic animal than the dog.

very troublesome, but it was imported as a favour by a French vessel. The common dock is also widely disseminated, and will, I fear, for ever remain a proof of the rascality of an Englishman, who sold the seeds for those of the tobacco plant " (Darwin's Voyage, 24th Dec. 1835).

[1] Both dogs and rats were introduced, and not indigenous to the island. "It is said the common Norway rat, in the short space of two years, annihilated in this northern end of the island, the New Zealand species " (Darwin's Voyage, 24th Dec. 1835).

In the marshes are found wild duck, teal, and blue fowl similar to but darker in hue than those of Madagascar, the Indies, and China. In the forests there are very beautiful wood pigeons about the size of a pullet, their sparkling blue and gold plumage is magnificent. These birds make splendid game. In the same forests are to be found very big parrots with black and variegated blue and red plumage, lories and a small variety of the latter with a very beautiful plumage similar to that of the lories of the island of Gola.[1]

The newly discovered lands abound with parson birds, starlings, pipits, the very common quail with the same plumage as our own but bigger, native robins of different colours, and birds like wagtails and wheatears.[2]

On the sea-coast one meets with many curlews, snipe, cormorants, black and white egrets similar to those of France, and a very beautiful black bird of the size of a sea-snipe, with bright red beak and feet.[3] With the exception of the egrets, whose flesh is very dry, all these birds are good to eat. The *envergures*, which the sailors call velvet cuffs, and grey and white gulls, are too dry, tough and oily to be eaten.[4]

From the day of our first landing I noticed that all the birds of this country were tame and allowed themselves to be approached so closely that they could be killed with stones and sticks; but when our young men had fired at them for a few days, the game became wild, although the savages could still approach closely, while they fled our sportsmen from afar off.

Fish are very abundant on this coast of New Zealand, and splendid *barbots*, mullet, and conger-eels are caught, as well as incredible quantities of mackerel much bigger than those from the coasts of France, but very good; many *balistes* of various colours, codfish in smaller quantities, two varieties of red fish like the gurnet which I have not met with elsewhere,

---

[1] Seven species of duck and eight of parrots are peculiar to New Zealand.
[2] There are no wagtails or wheatears in New Zealand.
[3] Probably the black stilt.
[4] For the birds of New Zealand, see Sir W. L. Buller's Birds of New Zealand, 2 vols. 4to. 1888. A splendid work.

and of which one variety is of about the size of a cod. All
these fish are good to eat. It appears that migratory fish are
to be met with on the coasts at different seasons of the year,
and I am convinced that the fishery must be much more
abundant in the straits which separate the two big islands of
this country.   In the rocks which fringe the coasts many
lobsters, crabs, and shellfish of every variety are to be met
with and similar to those which we found in Frederic Henry
Bay in Van Diemen's Land.[1]

We found neither penguins nor sea-wolves on this coast.
Out at sea at some distance from the land many whales and
white porpoises were seen, all of which could be hunted.

Departure from New Zealand, Continuation of the Voyage in the South Seas.

On the 14th July we left Treachery Bay, named Bay of
Islands on the chart by Captain Cook, and steered in a north-
easterly direction into the South Sea.   The wind was in
the S.E.   From the 16th to the 21st of July the wind
varied from N.E. to N.W., and we experienced violent winds
and a very heavy sea.   Up to the 25th the wind blew from the
S.W.   We found the winds variable and often contrary until
we had crossed the tropic of Capricorn.   We then met with
a clear sky and calm sea and wind from the S.E. to E.   Having
arrived at 20° S. latitude and longitude 185° E. of Paris, we
directed our course towards the east in search of the islands
Rotterdam and Amsterdam, which are marked on the chart in
the same latitude.   We navigated with the greatest care in
order not to pass these islands in the night.   On the 6th
of August we saw land ahead of us and approached it to within
two leagues.   The coast seemed fringed with breakers.   We
saw clearly a chain of low-lying islands, which looked like
beds of broken coral, on which Nature had planted a few

---

[1] For an account of the New Zealand fishes, see Fishes of New Zealand, by F.
W. Hutton, and Notes on Edible Fishes, by James Hector.   Published by the
Colonial Museum and Geological Survey (N.Z.) Department, 1872.

coco-nut palms ; the wind and current forced us on to the coast, but we searched in vain for an anchorage, the weather being bad and the sea rough. We stood off for the night, proposing to return in the morning and look for a roadstead.

On examining the excellent work of President de Brosses,[1] which I always had near me, I understood that the islands before us were not those of Rotterdam and Amsterdam which we were in search of, but a chain of coral islands to the north of the said islands. Having sounded several times without finding bottom, I changed the course for the north. When we were in sight of these rocks, we were in latitude 20° 9' S., and our longitude by reckoning was 182° E. of Paris, the variation being 11° 45' N.E. The islands of Rotterdam and Amsterdam should be placed in latitude 21° 80' as indicated on the chart.

In going north, we observed at daybreak on the 12th of August an island which I have not found on any chart, and I named it *Ile du point du jour* (Daybreak Island). It appeared to me an arid, steep, mountainous peak, surrounded by rocks, more especially on the south side, where they look very much like boats. I calculated it to be about five leagues in circumference. It is situated in 16° S. latitude, and according to our reckoning 182° 30' E. of Paris. On passing the island I found magnetic variation to be 8° 30' N.E.

The sight of this island did not cause us to deviate from our course. We had the finest of weather, with the wind E.S.E. On the 23rd August we crossed the line at 176° 43' E. longitude. From this point to the 8° N. latitude the variation was 10° to the N.E. The wind blew continuously from the S.E. From the time we saw the last islands we unceasingly met with land birds.

After the 28th of August, from N. latitude 8° to 13°, the wind veered about from W. to N. and to S.E. We now had very little wind, and the scurvy was playing havoc with our sailors, few being left in a state fit to work. This disease had made

[1] Charles de Brosses, 1709-1777. The first President of the Bourgogne Parliament, and a well-known historian. The work referred to here is his *Histoire des navigations aux Terres Australes*, 2 vols. 4to. Paris, 1756.

its appearance when we entered the tropics and had since then made rapid progress.

On the 2nd of September we changed our course to the W., the wind being constant from N.E. to E. We had rain occasionally, and continued to meet with indications of the neighbourhood of land until we sighted the island of Guam, the largest of the Marianne Islands,[1] on the 20th of September 1772, and where we anchored on the 27th of the same month.

ANCHORAGE AT THE ISLAND OF GUAM.

DESCRIPTION OF THE COUNTRY, AND OF THE SPANISH COLONY THERE.

We were much thwarted by winds on our land-fall at the island of Guam. After having beat to windward several days, the pilots came on board and steered us into the port, where we anchored in twenty fathoms on a mud bottom, the surface of which is covered with broken shells.

The harbour is situated on the western side, and almost in the middle of the island. It is bounded on the south by a tongue of land running two leagues out into the sea, and on the north by a reef of similar length, which almost surrounds it. The entrance is very narrow, and protected by a brick battery, which the Spaniards call St. Louis, mounted with eight bronze twelve-pounders of an old pattern. The harbour is capable of holding four vessels, sheltered from all winds except those from the south-east, which never blow but feebly in these parts. It

---

[1] So named in 1668, after Maria Anna of Austria, widow of Philip IV. of Spain. Magellan, who discovered the islands on 6th March, 1521, called them the Islas de los Ladrones, on account of the thieving propensities of the natives, who were, however, probably not worse in this respect than most of the Pacific islanders. This group has been frequently described, and amongst other voyagers who visited it were Cavendish, 1588; Dampier, 1686 and 1705; Wallis, 1768; and Freycinet in 1829 (Voyage autour du Monde, Paris, 4to. vol. ii. part 1. Historique). Dumont D'Urville visited it in 1828 and 1838. The Marianne islanders are Malayo-Polynesians, and skulls dug out of an ancient burial-ground on Guam show the same characteristics as those of the present aborigines (see Quatrefages and Hamy: Crania Ethnica, p. 455).

is dangerous to enter without pilots, because of the numerous
rocks and coral reefs.   It is situated in N. latitude 13° 26', and
longitude 141° 30' E. of Paris; the magnetic variation being
70° N.E.

The chief settlement, which the Spaniards call the town of
Agana, is situated four leagues to the north of the harbour on
the sea-coast, at the foot of some low mountains, in a beautiful
country full of springs, and watered by a small, very clear, and
good brook.   The Commandant of the island lives there.   The
streets of the town are laid out in straight lines, the private
houses are for the most part built solidly of wood, raised on
piles, about three feet above the level of the ground, and most
of them are roofed with shingles, or with tiles, the rest with
palm leaves.   There is a beautiful church highly decorated
according to Spanish custom.   The Commandant's house is
spacious and well built.   The former residence of the Jesuits,
now occupied by the St. Augustine brotherhood, is spacious
and convenient; but the former Jesuits' College, built for the
education of the Indians, is not inhabited, their successors,
the St. Augustines, having removed the college to a building
near their convent.   There is a barracks capable of lodging
a garrison of five hundred men, and there is the King's fine
large magazine.   All these public buildings are built of brick
and tile.   The island of Guam is the only island in the vast
extent of the South Sea, sprinkled as it is with innumerable
islands, which has a European built town, a church, fortifications, and a civilized population.

When we arrived at the town of Agana, we were received with
a great deal of civility by M. Tobias, the Commandant.   We
explained to him that our crews were suffering from scurvy,
and I asked him for help, which was all the more pressing,
as on our arrival we had not more than fifteen men fit for duty
in both vessels together.   This honourable and humane
Commandant began by sending on board a quantity of
provisions consisting of fresh meat, vegetables, and fruits,
especially of oranges and citrons.   He gave up to our use the
former Jesuits' College, he even allowed us to station a guard

6

to keep order, and he very civilly insisted that the officers of the two vessels should, during our stay at his island, make use of no other table than his own. We accepted with pleasure such very generous offers, which were made with the best possible grace. We had our unfortunate scurvy-stricken fellows brought on shore, and only left sufficient men in the vessels as were absolutely necessary for guarding them, and M. Tobias moreover furnished both vessels gratuitously with twenty-five Indians each as servants. With the abundant help we thus received from M. Tobias our sailors recovered rapidly.

In the whole extent of these seas there is no other harbour where weary navigators can re-establish their health more quickly or where they can obtain better or more abundant refreshment. The island of Guam appeared a terrestrial paradise to us ; the air was excellent, the water was very good, the vegetables and fruits perfect, the mobs of cattle as well as those of goats and pigs innumerable, while there was no end to the quantity of poultry.

However, things were not always so plentiful in Guam. When Magellan discovered it in 1521, together with eight other important islands lying to the north,[1] and a multitude of very much smaller islands, forming the little archipelago known first of all as the Ladrones and afterwards as the Mariannes Group, these islands, which were thickly inhabited, could only offer fish, bananas, coco-nuts, and breadfruit as refreshments to travellers, and these were only procurable by means of force against the arrows and blades of their savage inhabitants. The Spaniards brought from America the first stock of animals, of every variety of poultry, of the plants or fruit-seeds, as well as of the vegetables we find at the present day.

But this abundance, due to the care and genius of Europeans, has cost humanity very dear. The Ladrones, and especially Guam, were thickly populated when discovered, and it is said

[1] When Magellan departed from Guam on the 9th March, Master Andrew, of Bristol, the only Englishman in his fleet, died there (Guillemard's Life of Ferd. Magellan, London, 1890, p. 226).

that on the shores of Guam alone 20,000 inhabitants could be counted. These men were wild savages, and, like all the islanders of the South Sea, owing to the fact that they did not recognize any rights of property, they were great thieves.[1]

But they were so savage and so incapable of supporting the yoke of civilization that the Spainards who undertook to subdue them so as to make Christians of them saw their population annihilate itself so to speak within the course of two centuries. Under the reign of their missionaries the wild islanders were finally obliged to give way to the superiority of Spanish arms, and after having for a long time defended by cruel wars their right to exist like savage beasts, according to their free instinct, they gave themselves up to a despair of which there is no other example on the face of the earth. They induced their women to take drinks which caused abortion and to have no more children, rather than to leave behind them children who, according to the ideas of liberty entertained by these savage beings, would no longer be free. Such violent resolves, so contrary to the wishes of Nature, were followed up by a stubbornness in the nine Marianne Islands sufficient to reduce the population of the whole archipelago, which was 60,000 at the time of the discovery, to eight or nine hundred souls. About twenty years ago the scattered remnants of this population were gathered together by the Spaniards on to the island of Guam, where, during the last few years, by means of wise although tardy precautions of a Government perhaps best adapted to the climate of these islands and to the genius of the people, the population has commenced to increase.[2]

[1] The Marianne Islanders were perhaps not more given to petty pilfering from strangers than most of the South Sea Islanders. Cook had great trouble with regard to pilfering throughout his cruises, and La Perouse was not more fortunate, especially at Easter Island.

[2] It was not until 1695 that the islanders were finally subdued by the Spaniards and nominally converted to Christianity. They seem to have made a plucky resistance. A good account of the islands, of the customs and arts of the aborigines, and of the wars which led to their subjection, is to be found in the Histoire des Iles Marianes, 12mo. 433 pp. Paris, 1700, by Chas. Le Gobien, S.J., the great Chinese missionary.

The present remains of the former great population are descended from those Indians who, having attached themselves to the service of the Spaniards and especially to that of the missionaries, have allowed themselves to be domesticated by the mildness of the present government. All the others have disappeared without leaving any posterity.

The present population consists of about fifteen hundred Indians, They are happy under the government of a wise man, who has the good sense to see that religion is given to man for his happiness, even on earth, and not for his annoyance. It was with the greatest satisfaction that I saw this worthy and honourable man's only care was for the good of his island and that he never showed his authority except for the benefit of the Indians who serve him. Under such a Commandant even the monks appeared tolerant to me. The five or six Spaniards who have various subordinate posts under the chief conform perfectly to his views.[1]

[1] Anson's account of the Ladrones or Marianne Islands, where he landed in 1742, on Tinian Island, runs : "They were formerly most of them well inhabited, and, even not sixty years ago, the three principal islands Guam, Rota, and Tinian together, are said to have contained above fifty thousand people. But since that time Tinian hath been entirely depopulated, and only two or three hundred Indians have been left at Rota, to cultivate for the island of Guam ; so that now no more than Guam can properly be said to be inhabited. This island of Guam is the only settlement of the Spaniards ; here they keep a Governor and garrison, and here the Manilla ship generally touches for refreshment in her passage from Acapulco to the Philippines. It is estimated to be about thirty leagues in circumference, and contains by the Spanish accounts near four thousand inhabitants, of which a thousand are said to live in the city of San Ignatio de Agaña, where the Governor generally resides, and where the houses are represented as considerable, being built with stone and timber and covered with tiles, a very uncommon fabric for these warm climates and savage countries. Besides this city, there are upon the islands thirteen or fourteen villages. As this is a post of some consequence on account of the refreshment it yields to the Manilla ship, there are two castles on the sea-shore : one is the Castle of St. Angelo, which lies near the road, where the Manilla ship usually anchors, and is but an insignificant fortress, mounting only five guns, eight-pounders ; the other is the Castle of St. Louis, which is N.E. from St. Angelo, and four leagues distant, and is intended to protect the road where a small vessel anchors, which arrives here every other year, from Manilla. This fort mounts the same number of guns as the former. And besides these forts, there is a battery of five pieces of cannon on an eminence near the sea-shore. The Spanish troops employed on this island consist of three companies of foot, from forty to fifty men each ; and this is the principal strength the Governor has to

The greatest order reigns in Agana, and the country is really a delightful abode. Besides Agana there are twenty-one small Indian settlements round the islands, all on the sea-coast, and composed of five or six families each, who cultivate grain crops and vegetables, and occupy themselves with fishing.

The centre of the island still lies in its virgin state. The trees are not very high, but they are suitable for the building of houses and boats. The forests generally are very dense. Long ago the Spaniards cleared spaces of land for pastoral purposes. No other nation possessing colonies in the tropics appears to have laid themselves out like the Spaniards for the formation of savannahs. The whole art of this rural operation consists in making small clearings, which are only separated from each other by bushes and clumps of trees, simply cleared and cleaned of every variety of underwood. The Spaniards sow the clearings with varieties of grass seeds suitable for pasturage.

These savannahs, being shaded on all sides, always retain their freshness, and give shelter to the cattle against the sun and the great heat of the day. Vast prairies entirely cleared are not a success in the Torrid Zone, and cattle transferred from a colder climate only find the pasturage hard and burned by the power of the sun, being without any shade; and in cases where they are not able to rest during the greater heat of the day, they infallibly perish.

The cattle formerly transported from America to the savannahs of Guam and the other Ladrone Islands have multiplied without end. These animals have run wild, and now, when one wishes to eat them, one has either to shoot them or take them by lassooing. I noticed that the Guam cattle are generally white, with black ears, without any variety of colour, but with big frames and well nourished, and their flesh is very good to eat.

depend on; for he cannot rely on any assistance from the Indian inhabitants, being generally upon ill terms with them, and so apprehensive of them, that he has debarred them the use of fire-arms or lances." He complains that there are no good roadsteads at these islands (Anson's Voyage, London, 4to. 1748, pp. 337, 338).

The forests are also full of goats, pigs, and poultry, of which the first stock was brought over by the Spaniards. All these animals have run wild, and can only be obtained by shooting or running them down, or by lassooing. Their flesh is excellent.

Some time ago, M. Tobias brought over from the Philippines some stags and hinds, which have begun to multiply in the forest. These deer are as big as ours, but their coat is different. In Guam, from the month of December to May, the deer has a very long, thick, and grey coat; the hair is very thick round the neck of the animal, and forms a sort of hanging cravatte. In the month of May the deer puts on its summer coat, which is utterly different from that borne in winter. The hair is then fawn-coloured and almost yellow, smooth, and brilliant; there are three black stripes on its back, between which there are white stars, and one would say that it is not the same animal.

On the cleared lands and even in the interior of the forests an extraordinary quantity of turtle-doves, parrots, thrushes and blackbirds are met with.

Amongst the indigenous trees of the country one notices especially the coco-nut and the breadfruit trees. I observed three varieties of coco-nut palms: firstly the big common coco-nut palm similar to that which is found throughout the Indies, whose fruit furnishes a very pleasant, refreshing, anti-scorbutic milk, and spirit, oil, and a strong thread suitable for making up into twine, and even into ship's cables. Secondly the coco-nut palm, which may be called of medium size, because it does not grow so high as the other one, and whose nut, deprived of its fibrous husk and tender shell, is eaten like the heart of the artichoke, which it resembles. Finally, the black coco-nut, which does not grow above eight or ten feet high at most, although it grows much quicker than the common coco-nut palm, and the fruit of which is perfectly round and of the size of a six-pounder cannon ball; the flesh of this nut is much thicker and more delicate than that of the common coco-nut; spirit, oil, and thread are made from it in greater quantities than the others. The leaves of all three coco-nut palms are equally suitable for thatching houses and making mats.

The breadfruit tree is one of the most beautiful vegetable productions of Nature. It is a tall tree, of which the strong trunk grows straight upwards; its bark is perfectly smooth like that of our beeches. The branches do not start from the trunk until about the height of ten or twelve feet; they grow alternately, as do also the leaves. These leaves are generally eighteen inches to two feet long, very deeply indented like those of our French fig trees; they are stiff, thick, and of a very beautiful green, and form excellent food for cattle. With such a foliage the breadfruit tree affords the most perfect shelter. The fruit grows on the branches from the axil of the leaves, and attains the size of a *cantaloupe* melon, but more oval, and generally eight to ten inches long; it has a stalk proportioned to its size, and exactly resembles the jackfruit, which is known to all those who have journeyed to the Indies. Like the jackfruit it is covered with a thick skin, which is somewhat thorny, but of which the points are coarse, short, and blunted; its flower also resembles that of the jackfruit, but its pulp is different. That of the breadfruit tree is farinaceous, and of a taste which pleases all, even of those who eat it for the first time.[1] This fruit is one of the most useful presents which Nature has given to man, and it seems extraordinary that Nature should only have placed the tree which produces it in the islands of the South Seas. It tastes exactly like bread, has the same nutritive properties, supplies its place in every respect, and has a fragrant and delicious odour which our cleverest bakers will never be able to impart to our bread.

It is consequently very pleasant for the fortunate inhabitant of these islands, to be assured of his daily bread; to nourish himself he has only to cull it and eat it, and that too without any of the troubles attaching to ploughing the field, sowing the grain, hoeing, harvesting, threshing, winnowing, grinding, kneading, or baking.

---

[1] This account of the flavour of the breadfruit is exaggerated. Capt. Cook found it insipid.

The fruit can be eaten when it has attained its full size, but though it be still green. In this stage the islanders cook it before eating; they take off its knotty rind and cut it in slices like pieces of bread. When they wish to preserve it, they cut it in round slices, and in this very thin sea-biscuit form they dry it in the sun or in the oven. This natural biscuit preserves its quality for years, and very much better than does our ships' biscuit. Our sailors ate it green, slightly grilled; they also made their soup of it; they had no other bread, and we attributed the quick recovery of those suffering from scurvy to the bread-fruit diet. To this diet the inhabitants have always attributed anti-scorbutic properties.

When this fruit is ripe, it becomes yellow and soft, its odour is more fragrant, but it loses its farinaceous taste and becomes insipid. At this stage it has no longer the same properties as before; it is now laxative and heating; its pulp no longer takes the place of bread, and it has little to recommend it. Some of the breadfruit trees bear the male fruit and the others bear female fruit. In the latter, which are rare, the seed consists of shell-less stones enveloped in a simple almost cylindrical pellicle of about the size of a chestnut but longer. When ripe these stones make up for the uselessness of the pulp; they are cooked and eaten like chestnuts, having the same taste.

As the male breadfruit tree is the most useful, but has no seed, it is propagated by the Indians by making slight incisions in the roots, from which shoots spring up; these are transplanted together with a piece of the original root which has produced them.

It is very desirable that such a very useful tree should spread all over the earth. That there were some already in the Isle of France I knew well, thanks to M. Poivre, who during his administration collected with the greatest success all the most useful productions from the four corners of the globe. But as I was desirous of making common property of, and of multiplying as quickly as possible, such a very precious tree, I determined to fill a case of these plants in Guam and so to transport more to the Isle of France, thus placing the Governors in a position to encourage its planting in our other colonies, where the breadfruit tree alone without cultivation might furnish a very good food-substance, at least to our unhappy slaves. But I did not succeed as I had desired, and all but two of the plants perished.

The forests of Guam are full of guavas, several varieties of bananas, citrons, lemons, sweet, bitter and mandarin oranges, and breadfruits. The fruit of all these trees, which I presume are not indigenous to the island, but have been introduced by the Spaniards, are now-a-days so plentiful that they only cost the trouble of picking, and one finds them everywhere.

The sea-coast and the skirts of the forests are covered with a large variety of the caper tree. These small trees are indigenous to the soil. The Spaniards assure me that the nine Ladrone Islands were full of them when discovered, and that, like the breadfruit tree, they have been transplanted from here to the Philippines. Like the citrons, orange trees, and several other indigenous shrubs, these caper bushes flower all the year round, forming ravishing scenes; they exhale a pleasant odour, which makes a walk in the fields and in the forests very delicious.

Bananas are found throughout the world between the tropics and as far as the Cape of Good Hope in latitude 33° S. As several travellers have described them and their varieties, I will not repeat the descriptions here, but I noticed at Guam two varieties which deserve attention, and which I believe are peculiar to the Marianne Islands as well as to the Philippines, where the Spaniards assure me they have them also.

The first species is a dwarf banana, which does not grow higher than three feet; in its leaves, which are in proportion to its height, as well as in the substance of its trunk and in its flower, it resembles the generality of all banana trees, but its fruit is different, and very superior in taste to all the bananas known in other parts of the world. It produces a very thick perfectly round stalk, carrying five or six hundred fruits pressed closely together, every fruit about the size of an almost round nut, and covered with a very fine skin which yellows or reddens in ripening, for it is of either colour, and which is easily separated from the enclosed pulp. This fruit has not the fault common to other bananas of being clammy or dry; it is watery, with a very delicious taste, slightly acid, and scented. It is very superior, even to the little yellow banana known in the East Indies as the *Gengi* fig, which is truly delicate, but the one of which I am now speaking is beyond compare the best banana that I have ever eaten. This excellent fruit ought certainly to be transplanted into all our tropical colonies, and it certainly deserves the preference to all other varieties of banana, quite as much for its diminutiveness as for the excellence of its fruit, and should be cultivated in our hot-houses, where until now only the bad variety has been grown, and the fruit of which is not even eaten there where Nature originally placed it.

The second species is a wild variety, which grows taller than any of the others, and of which the trunk is thicker, it has also a more uncultivated appearance. Its leaves and flowers resemble those of all bananas, and its fruit is not edible, being nothing more than a mass of grain bound together by a very poor pulp which has a sharp and disagreeable taste. The trunk of this wild banana is of the greatest use to those who cut it down and steep it, on account of the quantity of thread which it furnishes. The entire trunk consists of nothing more than a mass of very long and strong threads, and of which the Indians make cloth, cord, and even cables for the galleons of Acapulco.[1] This wild banana is locally called *abaca*. The Spaniards, who have put such cables to the proof, maintain that, the thickness being equal, they are stronger than the hempen European cables, and resist the action of wind and salt-water better, especially for the bow anchor. This variety of banana has already been largely propagated at the Isle of France, and deserves to be transplanted to all our colonies. It is well known that bananas can be propagated without end and without cultivation. The *abaca* multiplies still more rapidly, and every

---

[1] Acapulo, a beautiful land-locked harbour in Mexico (N. lat. 16° 50', W. long. 99° 52'), which for many years after its discovery was the point of annual departure of the Spanish Treasure Fleet to the Philippines. Although for a time it fell into decay, it still remains an important port on the Pacific coast of America.

trunk one year old gives ten to twelve pounds of thread suitable for making into rope.

The rivers of Guam, which after all are only brooks, or torrents, abound in fish. During their convalescence, our sailors amused themselves by fishing, and caught eels, mullets, gobys, and a sort of carp. All these fish are excellent, but the Indians do not eat them, preferring salt-water fish, which are generally very inferior in quality to the fresh-water ones. It is true that the abundance of meat, vegetables, and fruit is so great in Guam, and the Spanish Commandant provided us with them so generously, that during the whole stay we hardly thought of getting any sea-fish.

There is, besides, some inconvenience in a preference for salt-water fish. Among those which are caught on the coast of Guam, as in all the Marianne Islands, there are some which are very unwholesome, for they nourish themselves on the little polypes, which form the coral. It appears that these sea-insects, like the sea-galleys and sea-nettles, have some caustic property which is imparted to the fishes, and the fishes have a coralline taste which betrays their poisonous properties. The Indians know which are unwholesome, but it is better not to eat any sea-fish at all. This, however, does not hold good with the sea-turtles which are caught on the coasts of Guam. They are very good and as big as those of the island of Ascension, but the Spaniards and Indians do not eat them. I collected sufficient to form a good supply during our journey to the Philippines.

The Agriculture and Arts of the Guam Indians.

Before the arrival of M. Tobias, the Indians did not occupy themselves with any sort of cultivation on a large scale, for the galleons brought thither the requisite flour for the bread of the missionaries and of the garrison; but the Jesuits, who were in charge of the mission, cultivated a few fruit trees and vegetables, while the Indians lived on breadfruit and sea-fish.

The new Commandant, believing that one of the best measures for re-establishing the almost annihilated population of the

Mariannes, reduced to a mere handful of inhabitants collected together at Guam, would be by making the little colony into an agricultural one, introduced the cultivation of rice, maize, indigo, cotton, cacao, and sugar cane, all of which have succeeded very well. The cultivation of maize especially gives incredible results. It is common to find on the maize fields plants twelve feet high, with eight to ten cobs, nine to ten inches long, well stocked with good nourishing grain. The Indian reduces the maize to flour and makes bread of it.

M. Tobias has also established cotton mills and salt pans on his island; in a word, he has awakened industry in this little people, whom he could not better civilize than by procuring them new gratifications and wants and tastes for industry.

His views have led him to establish a public free school for the Indian children, where they are taught reading, writing, and arithmetic, and vocal and instrumental music. There is a school for the boys and a separate one for the girls. It was always a new and pleasant surprise to us when we attended divine service on Sundays and holidays to find the church full of musicians, and to hear all the instruments in tune and time.

Under the guidance of this wise man all the Indians have become agriculturists. Every family has its property, which is divided into gardens, orchards, and ploughed or spade-worked fields. Every variety of European vegetables, especially delicious melons, and the very refreshing water-melons, are found in these gardens. Ships wishing to provision will find cabbages and gourds in very large quantities.

The orchards are full of mangoes and pine apples, and every fruit tree of which I have spoken is to be found in the fields and right up into the forests; but the cultivated trees give the best and most abundant fruit, especially as regards the mangoes, which have been brought from Manilla, and are of a very superior quality. The mango is one of the best fruits in the world and one can eat many of them without being inconvenienced!

In order to set the example in agricultural matters the Commandant has himself laid out some very pleasant gardens;

he has had avenues of coco-nut palms and breadfruit trees four deep planted along the sea-shore round the town, and in public spaces, and these avenues have made Agana an enchanting place.

To facilitate work in connection with cultivation and land transport, the Government has built good roads and has imported horses from Manilla, and donkeys and even mules from Acapulco. The Indians have been taught to break-in cattle and to use them as draughts, and as the variety of cattle are big and strong, they make very fine teams. The Indians have more particularly succeeded in accustoming the cattle to carry them, the same as horses do, and there are no Indians who have not several riding beasts on which they ride when making a journey into the interior of the islands and on whom they saddle their baggage. In their method of breaking-in they follow the Malabar custom ; they pierce the nostril of the beast and pass the end of a cord through it, and by means of this cord, to which the cattle get accustomed in a fortnight, they are led about as easily as horses by their bridles.

The art of cultivation in its turn causes the birth of the art of the smith, of the wheelwright, of the joiner and carpenter. The Indians of Guam have learnt all these trades and follow them with great skill ; they make bricks and lime, and are even good masons.

In establishing the useful arts on his island M. Tobias has not neglected that particular one which is unfortunately necessary for safety and defence : and he has formed an Indian militia two hundred strong, which wears a uniform and is well paid. The militiamen are under the command of four Spanish captains. The other officers are mostly mestizos and Indians from the Philippines. I thought these troops performed their duties well; but the Commandant, regarding indolence as one of the greatest disadvantages of life, has continued his men as cultivators without in the least interfering with their daily duties, employing them in cultivating certain lands which he has divided off under the title of Royal Demesnes. The soldiers thus plough, sow, and harvest the lands, the produce of which serves to nourish them, and being thus always occupied, they are happy and well contented with the rice, or the bread made from the maize, which they have themselves cultivated and harvested.

In acquiring new knowledge by their contact with civilization, the islanders have at the same time preserved perfectly the art of making canoes received from their forefathers. In this respect they had nothing new to learn. It is quite certain that the invention of the form of their craft would do honour to any boatbuilder amongst the most advanced maritime people. This form has not been copied from any model, for it differs from all those which have been given to sea-going vessels by any of the known peoples in different parts of the world.

The Indians being of one nationality, but divided up amongst nine very thickly populated islands, and separated from one another by considerable distances within an extent of about six degrees, naturally require good boats wherewith to inter-communicate. As the islands are situated in a row running north and south, and as the wind blows from the east almost all the year round, it is an advantage that their boats should have no stern. Their boats are therefore built with bows at each end, so that they never require to be turned round. The prevailing winds blow sometimes very violently in squalls, and the islanders have found out how to provide against this inconvenience, for they furnish their boats with outriggers, which will uphold them against the stiffest breezes and the biggest waves. These canoes, always having the wind on one side, are built flat on that, the windward, side and rounding on the lee side, which, being more under water, requires a more suitable surface for cutting through the water. The mast is never placed in the middle of the boat, but on the curved lee side, so that the mast is, so to speak, between the boat and the outrigger. The weight of the mast thus causes the side to list, and with all the more ease, since the windward side of the boat being flat offers less resistance. Nothing is so simple or so well devised as these boats, which the Indians call *proas*.

The outrigger is composed of four pieces of wood, built oblong in form, and of which the longest side is set parallel with the round side of the boat. At the beam ends of the outrigger is fixed a large piece of very light wood cut in the shape of a canoe. This piece of wood floats on the water and opposes such resistance to the efforts of the strongest breezes as to prevent the upsetting of the boat; the arms of the outrigger are fixed at right angles into the upper planks of the boat, and strongly tied on to the planks on the windward side. Three pieces of wood cross the framework and make it firmer, and two other longer pieces which cross the framework transversely, that is, parallel with the boat and its outrigger, help to bind the whole firmly together. A narrow plank is placed along the lee rail to prevent the water entering the boat, and fixes still more securely in their position the arms of the outrigger, which it does by covering its whole length.

On the arms of the outrigger and partly on the lee rail, the Indians rig up a platform, which is again a source of strength, and acts as a sort of counter-weight to the boat. The boatmen and the passengers sit on this platform and the cargo is placed there.

The mast is of bamboo and is consequently very light. It is let into a socket on the lee side of the bottom of the boat. Two stays from each end of the boat keep it in its place, a shroud holds it on the windward side and another on the leeward side; the latter is lashed to the framework of the outrigger, and the mast is further shored up by a bamboo fixed in the middle of the outrigger.

The boat is furnished with a triangular mat sail, furnished with a yard and boom. The boom is supported at its base in the boat by a semicircular socket; there is one of these at either end of the boat. When the Indians, troubled by contrary winds, wish to tack about, they run the end of the boom along the flat side of the boat, and fix it in the opposite socket at the other end; then in changing the boom, end for end, the stern of the boat becomes its prow, and the tack is accomplished. When the wind is too strong and the Indians wish to shorten sail, they simply roll it round the boom, and so diminish the exposed surface.

The boat I observed was forty feet long by three broad; the bottom was made of a single hollow tree, in the form of a big canoe; its sides raised a couple of inches by means of planks and sewn together with bark of trees and caulked with a mixture of coco-nut oil and quicklime. Their sides were joined by cross-pieces, which served as seats. These boats have no bridge, neither have they any rudder; an Indian squatted at the end of the boat governs it with a very broad-bladed paddle.

I made a short passage in one of these proas when the wind was fresh, and estimated its speed at three leagues an hour. The islanders assured me that with a very strong wind they could go five leagues an hour, but that such speed was rarely attained. These proas are therefore the best sailers amongst the small sea-going craft known, and are very ingeniously constructed. It appeared to me that those of Guam are not quite safe at sea, for a wave might detach the outrigger or break it, and the boat would then capsize or founder; but I have been assured that the Indians are such good swimmers, and so experienced in their art of navigation, that when a boat capsizes through the loss of its outrigger, they have sufficient skill to right it in the open sea, and they never lose more than their cargo. It has been found possible elsewhere to give the proas greater solidity, preserving at the same time their form and swiftness, and boats uniting these advantages are found on the coast of Cochin China.[1]

---

[1] Dumont D'Urville (Voy. de l'Astrolabe, vol. v. p. 262) mentions on his first visit to the Marianne Islands, May, 1828, that the natives were then no longer able to make these canoes, and those from the Carolines, constructed on like principle, were used instead. Vice-Admiral E. Paris, who was a midshipman with D'Urville, tells me (Aug. 1888) this statement is quite correct. For the best description of these proas, see Appendix, where Anson's detailed account, with plan, is given. Captain Woodes Rogers, who visited Guam in 1710, was so pleased as a seaman with the speed and handiness of the proas of Guam, that he carried one of them to London, thinking it might be worth fitting up there as a curiosity on the Canal in St. James's Park (R. C. Leslie, Life Aboard a British Privateer, London, 1889).

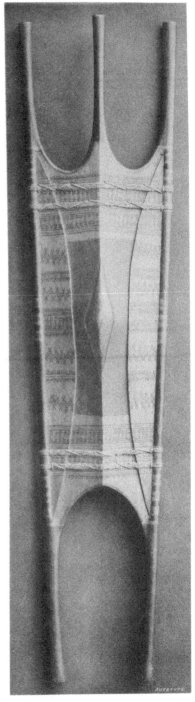

CONTINUATION OF VARIOUS OBSERVATIONS MADE AT GUAM.

According to the estimates of the Spaniards, the island of Guam is about forty leagues in circumference. From the sea-shore it rises by very slow degrees towards its centre, but it is not mountainous. The inhabitants maintain that the soil is everywhere good and fertile, with the exception of the northern portion, which forms a peninsula, and is only slightly watered, the rest of the island being well watered, and one cannot go a league in any direction without coming across a stream. Towards the interior of the country, east and south of Agana, there are many fresh-water springs issuing out of the rocks, and which form at intervals pools of clear water, which, being shaded by bushy trees, maintain a most refreshing coolness in spite of the great heat of the climate.

The island is studded with picturesque and delicious scenes. In my promenades it often happened that I came across these enchanting places where Nature had made all, and the hand of man none of, the arrangements. It was not possible to feel bored, everything was arranged for the happiness of the man who loves solitude, verdure, shade, freshness, the smell of flowers, crystalline water springing from a rock and falling in cascades; who enjoys the songs of numberless birds, and glimpses of scenery, coco-nuts, breadfruits, oranges, citrons, and an infinity of wild fruits found equally on trees with their flowers, and growing in that charming irregularity in which art has never been able to imitate Nature. It was only with regret that I could leave such delicious places, for I could have spent my whole life there. Between these delightful spots and the sea-coast there is an open space, about two hundred fathoms broad, consisting of sand mixed with coral, which appears to have been abandoned by the sea, or to have emerged from its bosom by the effect of some volcanic shock or upheaval. These lands consist of a series of valleys perfectly filled up with coral, and which appear to have been formerly the beds of marine currents. One has to pass three or four of these dales one after another

7

before arriving at the vegetable soil of the island on the skirts of the forest. All this space is full of uncultivated growth, of caper trees and coco-nut palms, which thrive well in the midst of the coral.

It appeared to me that the greater part of the rocks around Agana are granitic; the pebbles which are found on the sea-shore are crystallized inside. I noticed that amongst the small pyramidal crystals enclosed in these pebbles there were some which were yellow and red, like topazes and rubies.

The Guam islanders are such as they were depicted by Magellan: short in stature, ugly enough, black, and generally scabby, although they bathe frequently. The women are generally beautiful, well made, and with a red skin. Both men and women have very long hair. Through civilization this small people have become hospitable, honest, and peaceful; at the same time they have adopted a vice unknown to their ancestors, for the men are slightly given to drunkenness, and will drink a great deal of coco-nut spirit. They love music and dancing, but do not care much about work. They are passionately fond of cock-fighting. On Sundays and holidays they assemble after service at the door of the church, every man bringing his cock to fight that of another, and every man bets on his own bird.

The Guam Mission is at the present day in the hands of the St. Augustines, who have replaced the Jesuits, and there are five of the brotherhood attached to the Mission. One of them is appointed to the parish of Agana, three of them are divided between different parishes among other tribes in the Island, and the fifth inhabits the Island of Saipan, which is ten leagues to the north of Guam, and where a small population has been located.

These good monks thoroughly second the views of M. Tobias for the welfare of his beloved Indians. I cannot repeat too often, in praise of this excellent man, that he has no other ambition than that of making his islanders happy; and that he is happy himself because he succeeds in all his views. The Indians look upon him and love him as a father. He has often repeated to me that he should like to finish his days in

Guam, calling my attention to the fact that in no other part of the world could he be happier, since he had the satisfaction of seeing a small tribe confided to his care, in the enjoyment of a very good climate and of an abundance of all the productions of the earth.[1]

We had landed with more than two hundred sick men at Guam, and we had not lost a single one of them; all had completely recovered within the space of a month, in spite of the almost continual rains we had to put up with, until towards the middle of October. The northern monsoon, which commenced at this period, brought us fine weather and a clear sky, and we profited by the occasion to repair our vessels.

During our abode at Guam I noticed that at the change of the moon the sea grew very rough for two or three days. After a rest of about two months, we were disposed to profit by the N.E. monsoon in order to get to the Philippine Islands. On the 18th of November we took on board both our vessels abundant provisions, so generously furnished us by M. Tobias; these consisted of beef, pigs, goats, poultry, vegetables and fruit of every description. We had paid four piastres for the bullocks, but were not allowed to pay for any other provisions. M. Tobias furnished us with a pilot to guide us into the Philippine Archipelago.

---

[1] La Perouse, who was in Manilla from 28th Feb. to 9th April, 1787, says (Voyage Round the World, 3 vols. 8vo. London, 1807): "I saw at Manilla that upright and virtuous Governor of the Ladrones, M. Tobias, who, unhappily for his repose, has been too much celebrated by Abbé Raynal. I saw him persecuted by the monks, who, representing him as a wretch, destitute of piety, have alienated the affections of his wife, who has even demanded to be separated from him, that she might not live with a pretended reprobate, and all the fanatics have applauded her resolution. M. Tobias is lieutenant-colonel of the regiment which forms the garrison at Manilla, and is known to be the best officer in the country; yet the Governor has ordered that his appointments, which are considerable, should be paid to this pious wife, leaving him only twenty-six dollars per month for his own subsistence and that of his son. This brave soldier, reduced to despair, was waiting for a proper opportunity to quit the colony in order to obtain justice" (vol. ii. ch. v. p. 285). When Dumont D'Urville visited Guam in 1828, he found every sign of a rapid decay, but on his second visit, ten years later, under a new Governor, it seemed to have recovered somewhat.

DEPARTURE FROM THE ISLAND OF GUAM AND CONTINUATION
OF OUR JOURNEY TO THE PHILIPPINE ISLANDS.

We left Agana with deep regret on the 19th of November,
but with a good north-easterly wind, and our sailors, who were
in better health than they would have been even in leaving
a French port, called the island a terrestrial paradise. Our
course lay W. by a quarter N.W. in order to get into the Strait
of San Bernardino, which is the ordinary course for galleons on
returning from Acapulco to Manilla. On the 20th, at two
o'clock in the afternoon, the *Mascarin* sprang a leak forward,
below the lower deck in the starboard bow, which we were
unable to stop, and she made water at the rate of six inches
an hour. During the whole of our journey from Guam until we
sighted Catanduanes, to the east of Luzon, and to the north of
the Straits of San Bernardino, we had easterly and north-easterly
winds; when the wind was in the east, we had fine weather
and a calm sea; and when the wind was in the north, we
had strong squalls, rain, and a heavy sea, and thunder and
lightning.

On the 27th and 28th of November we had spread but little
sail, on account of the rough weather, and we kept head to wind
during two nights, because, according to our reckoning and to
the Spanish Chart of Father Mourillo, we should have been
on the coast of the Isle of Luzon since the 27th; by
M. d'Après'[1] chart we were, according to our reckoning, five
leagues off at noon on the 28th. However that may be, and
although the horizon was very clear, we did not discover
land that day, and we kept head to wind again on the night
of the 28th and 29th. It seems that there is a strong
easterly current in the different straits in the stretch of sea
which separates the Philippines from the Marianne Islands.

---

[1] Après de Mannevillette, 1707–1780. A well-known hydrographer, who
published a series of charts chiefly relating to the Indies and China, under the
title *Neptune Oriental*. He was also chief of the French Company's Institute in
Paris, which was a sort of depôt for charts and the dissemination of information
relating to the Indies.

At daybreak on the 29th we made land without being able to distinguish it well; the tide was making and the waves made a noise like that of breakers. At six o'clock in the morning we sighted distinctly the northern part of the island of Catanduanes, which appeared to me to be ten leagues off. This part of the island is high, mountainous, and covered with trees. At seven o'clock we sighted the easternmost point of Luzon, called Montafou on the charts, then the little island of San Bernardino, which appeared to be barren and surrounded with breakers, and which at eight o'clock in the morning was three leagues off to the S.S.E. This island is three hundred and seventy-seven leagues distant from Guam, and according to my observation it is situated in latitude 12° 44′ N. and longitude 121° 13′ east of Paris; magnetic variation was 1° N.E. On entering the straits, we saw the Island of Samar very clearly, it appeared to be low, rocky, covered with trees, and surrounded by islets.

We did not see Cape Spiritto Santo, which is the N.E. point of the island of Samar, where the galleons returning from Acapulco land during the S.E. monsoon. It was at this cape that M. Anson established his quarters for his attack on the Manilla galleon, which he had the good fortune to take in June, 1743.[1]

The Island of San Bernardino is situated in the middle of the straits bounded to the north by the S.E. point of Luzon, and the N.E. point of Samar Island; the channel is four leagues broad here, and six leagues broad between the cape of Samar Island and the Island of San Bernardino. With the winds of the northern monsoon we entered the north channel by coasting along Bulusan, on the Island of Luzon. The galleons which enter this strait during the S.W. monsoon pass through the channel between Samar and San Bernardino.

As soon as we had passed this little island, which we left

---

[1] On the 26th of August, 1742, Captain Anson sent a cutter on shore at the island of Tinian, not far from Guam. Here his ship, the *Centurion*, was refitted, and from here she re-started on her memorable voyage when she took the Spanish galleon *Nostra Seigniora de Cabadonga*. See Anson's Voyage, 4to. London, 1748, p. 304.

on our S.E., we encountered such a very strong south-westerly current that we could hardly manage our vessels. In coasting along Luzon we saw to the west of San Bernardino the settlement of Bulusan, in which I noticed a big building which might be a church. We hoisted our ensign, and were immediately answered by the Spaniards. This coast is pleasant to look at, with easily accessible sand coves and several fresh-water creeks.

At two o'clock we found ourselves two leagues off the northern point of the Island of Capul. This island is the only one on the whole route off which we could, so to speak, anchor in the open sea. The bottom for three leagues gave us very unequal soundings, but we found it good at 70 to 35 fathoms, although we did not begin to reach it until the Island of San Bernardino was five leagues to our N.E. At the same time the islands of the Cape of Bulusan were to the N. of us, and the northern point of Capul was to our S. We found no bottom when the same point was four leagues E.S.E. of us.

During the night we had little wind and less current. On the 30th November we continued our journey up the mid channel between the Island of Ticao and Luzon. In passing the head of the north of Ticao I noticed the settlement of Colentas, which appeared to be tolerably large. The church was especially striking. Throughout this journey we did not find bottom at one hundred fathoms, and we passed, on the north of the Island of Luzon, the beautiful port Sol-Sogou, of which the Island of Bagatao forms the entrance. As soon as we had passed the little islands at the N. of Ticao, we made for the S.E. point of the Island of Bourias, which we coasted for a league, leaving the northern point of Masbate Island, which is three times as big, about two leagues to the south.

The passage amongst these islands could not possibly be more beautiful; there is no danger and one can beat about everywhere, although it is true there is no bottom except close to the shores. On the 1st of December the wind fell, and with it came rain and thunder, and we made little progress. On the 2nd, the sea having calmed down, we saw the little Island of Bancou five leagues to the W.S.W. At one o'clock, having sighted the

Island of Marindonqué, we steered W.S.W. in order to coast the southern point, and so avoid striking the Two Hermanas, or the Two Sisters, which are on the N.W. of Bancou Island. In this passage, which is about five leagues broad, the currents carried us rapidly along on to the island of Mindoro, but we recovered by tacking about. The southern point of Marindonqué is terminated by a large islet. On coasting the eastern side of this island we found, at two leagues from the coast, three islets, which the Spaniards have named the Viregos, the Viceroys, which we doubled a league off.

On leaving these islands, we had been obliged to tack, so that we might go N.N.W. and N.W. in order to gain Point Galbau, on the Island of Luzon, and pass between Calampau and Green Island. Calms, rains and squalls followed alternately. On the 3rd December we reached the coast of Luzon, and passed between this island and Green Island. I noticed that the latter island has breakers on the S.E. side, and I should prefer the two-leagues-wide passage between Luzon and Green Island to that which appears bigger between the latter island and Mindoro. The latter passage is endangered by several islets, although it is said that this is the passage used by the galleons on their way from Manilla through the Straits of San Bernardino to Acapulco. Since we arrived in the Philippine Archipelago I have observed that there was no magnetic variation. All these islands are well wooded, look pleasant, and have plenty of streams.

On the 4th of December, having doubled Green Island, and the wind having veered to the S.E., we steered for Mindoro, passing the southern point of the Island of Maricaban a league off. In the afternoon we had a clear view of Callavitte Point, to the N. of Mindoro, the coast of Luzon, San-Jago Point, Taal Lagoon, and Loubang, and the Goats and Fortune Islands. Contrary winds detained us in this passage, which is not without its dangers. During the night, in spite of the strong S.E. currents which carried us on to the dangerous islands of Ambil, Loubang and the Goats, we safely passed Fortune Island a league off to the W.

The next morning, the 5th of December, we had to tack about

to gain the entrance to Manilla Bay. We had anchored the night before on a good thirty fathom black sand bottom outside the Island of Marivelles, about two leagues off. After experiencing three calm days and three days with contrary winds, we entered the bay by the southern passage of Marivelles Island, and anchored on the 8th in Port Cavitte, in a three-and-a-half fathom mud bottom. There we met the Spanish frigate *Venus*, commanded by M. Langara,[1] who was preparing to return to Spain *viâ* the Cape of Good Hope. We also found the galleons *St. Joseph* and *St. Charles*, with several other craft and galleys.

ANCHORAGE IN MANILLA BAY.

DESCRIPTION OF PORT CAVITTE AND OF WHAT WE DID THERE.

Manilla Bay is almost quite round; it is about seven leagues across in every direction, and twenty leagues in circumference from point to point. It has a S.E. aspect. Marivelles Island is situated in the middle of the entrance, and is half a league broad by two long, and forms N. and S. passages. Both these passages are equally good. The passage on the S., which appears to be broadest, is somewhat contracted by two islets, or rocks, one of which, called Le Fraisé, is on the Luzon side, and the other, called Monja, is close to Marivelles Island. On this island the Spaniards have established an Indian post to give notice of vessels in search of the entrance to the harbour. When they see a ship, they hoist a flag, discharge a mortar, and some of them immediately take a boat for Cavitte and Manilla, to give notice of what they have sighted. The distance from Marivelles to Cavitte is about seven leagues.

This port is situated in the S.E. corner of the bay; it is horseshoe in form, and will hold twelve ships, which are safe on a mud bottom. It is defended by a large battery and a small fort.

---

[1] Don Juan de Langara, 1730–1800, was a Spanish Admiral, who distinguished himself greatly at the battle of St. Vincent in 1780, where he was taken prisoner by Admiral Rodney.

The Spaniards have established a staff of officers here, under the orders of a commandant, called a Castillano; they have a major, an adjutant, a sub-adjutant and a commander of artillery, and three hundred men in garrison. There is also an arsenal with all its workshops surrounded by walls, magazines and a dockyard. On the tongue of land on the W. side of the port there is a fairly big village, peopled by sailors and every description of Indian workmen employed in the repairing and careening of vessels. The village contains about a thousand souls and has three churches. The city of Manilla is situated three leagues and a half from Cavitte, and almost in the middle of the eastern portion of the bay.

After having paid the necessary visits at Cavitte, and having taken proper precautions in the port for the safety of our vessels, we went to Manilla, to the Governor-General, who received us extremely well and afforded us all the help we asked for to enable us to repair our vessels. From the palace of the Governor we went to that of the Archbishop, who received us with every possible mark of kindness. We then made the other customary visits to the members of the Royal Audience, to the principal officers of the place, and to the chief citizens.

A few days afterwards I took up my abode in a suburb which is called Saint Croix, where strangers generally lodge. Communication between the land and our ships by means of boats was so easy, that our work did not suffer in the slightest by our establishment in this Manilla suburb. In the meanwhile I did not lose a moment in stopping the *Mascarin's* leak, which had sprung during our journey from Guam.

Having dismantled this storeship, and having cleared away some of the sheathing in search of the leak, I found that the vessel required far greater repairs than I had at first thought necessary. Her examination being completed, it was decided to refit her, which I did at once, changing some rotten planks, some essential portions of her bows, and a large topmast, which were past service. But all these repairs took a long while to do, because our best sailors deserted day by day, and because the native Indian workmen do not work quickly.

On the 15th February, 1773, the *Castries*, entirely remasted and careened, commanded by Chevalier Duclesmeur, weighed anchor in Manilla Bay in order to profit by the N.E. monsoon to return to the Isle of France, the deserters being replaced by twenty Indian sailors. I remained behind to complete the refitting and re-equipping of the *Mascarin*, which was done on the last day of February.

On the 1st of March I cleared Port Cavitte, and anchored at the mouth of the Manilla river in four and a half fathoms with a mud bottom. This anchorage is a mile away from the mouth of the river, and formed by two stone jetties which extend three cables' lengths from the shore. I approached close to the city, for at this season of the year no squalls are to be feared, so as to be able to ship my stores more promptly and at less cost. I made several attempts to get back my deserted sailors, but I perceived clearly that they had been seduced from their duties, they as well as those of the *Castries*, and even those of the Spanish frigate, which had been obliged to leave the bay on its return to Spain with fifty Indian sailors to replace the same number of Spanish sailors whom the Governor was suspected of having prevailed upon to desert, and who had all put in an appearance at Cavitte the morning after the departure of the frigate. I was obliged to give way to superior force, and engaged thirty Indian boatmen to replace my deserters. They demanded, as a condition of their engagement, that I should give them two months' pay in advance. I was forced to concede this demand, and some of them then deserted with their pay. They might perhaps all have deserted, had I not on my part, in engaging them, taken the precaution to retain them on board, and not allowing them to land again unless they left another man as substitute.

On the 8th of March all my stores were on board. I had said good-bye to the Governor and to everybody in the place, and I only awaited a favourable wind to weigh anchor and return to the Isle of France. Before leaving this harbour I will here note down my observations on Manilla, and on the colony of which it is the capital.

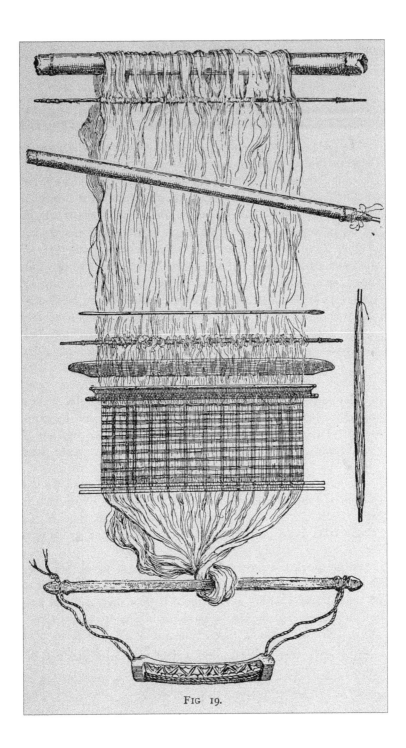

FIG 19.

OBSERVATIONS MADE AT MANILLA, THE CAPITAL OF THE
PHILIPPINES.

The city of Manilla is one of the most beautiful that Europeans
have built in the East Indies; its houses are all of stone, with tile
roofs and they are big, comfortable and well ventilated. The streets
of Manilla are broad and perfectly straight; there are five principal
streets, which divide the city lengthwise, and about ten which
divide it broadways. The form of the city is that of an oblong,
surrounded by walls and ditches, and defended on the side of
the river by a badly-planned citadel, which is about to be pulled
down and rebuilt. The city walls are flanked by a bastion at
every one of the four angles. There are at Manilla eight principal churches, with an open place in front of every one; they
are all beautiful, large and very richly decorated. The Cathedral
is a building which would grace any of our chief European cities,
and has just been rebuilt by an Italian Theatin,[1] who is an able
architect. The two rows of columns which support the vaults
of the nave and of the aisles are of magnificent marble, so also
are the columns of the portal, the altars, the steps and the pave-
ment. These marbles are obtained from local quarries, are of
great variety, and are of the greatest beauty. The space in front
of the Cathedral is very large, and is the finest in the city.

On one side the Palace of the Governor is flanked by the
Cathedral, on the other by the Town Hall. The Town Hall is
very beautiful. At the extremity of the place in front of the
Cathedral a large barracks is being constructed, and which is to
be capable of lodging eight thousand troops.

Private houses, as well as public buildings, are all one story
high. Spaniards never live on the ground floor, on account of
the dampness, but they occupy the first floor instead. The heat
of the climate has induced them to build very large apartments,
with verandahs rnnning right round the outside, so as to keep
out the sun; the windows form part of the verandahs, and the

---

[1] A regular order of clergy established at Rome in 1524, but which does not
appear to have spread much beyond Italy and France.

daylight only enters the rooms by means of the doors which open out on to these verandahs. The ground floor serves as a storehouse, and to prevent the rising of moisture from the soil its surface is raised a foot, by means of a bed of charcoal; then sand or gravel is placed on the top of this bed, which is finally paved with stone or brick laid with mortar.

As the country is very subject to earthquakes, the houses, although built of stone, are strengthened with large posts of wood or iron fixed perpendicularly in the ground, rising to the top of the wall-plates, and built within the walls, so that they cannot be seen, and then crossed on every floor by master girders, strongly bound together and bolted by wooden keys, and which so consolidate the whole building.

Manilla is built on the mouth of a beautiful river, which flows from a lake, called by the Spaniards *Lagonne-de-bay*, and which is situated five leagues inland. Forty streams flow into this lake, which is twenty leagues in circumference, and around which there are as many villages as streams. The Manilla river is the only one which flows out of the lake. It is covered with boats, bringing to the city every sort of provision from the forty agricultural tribes established on the lake shores.

The suburbs are bigger and more thickly populated than the city itself; they are separated from it by a river, across which a beautiful bridge has been thrown. The Minondo suburb is more especially inhabited by half-breeds, Chinese and Indians, who are for the most part gold and silversmiths, and all of them workpeople.

The Saint Croix suburb is inhabited by Spanish merchants, by foreigners of all nations, and by Chinese half-breeds. This quarter is the most agreeable one in the country, because the houses, which are quite as fine as those of the city, are built on the river bank, and thereby they enjoy all the conveniences and pleasantness due to such a position.

In spite of such advantages, the city is badly situated, being placed between two intercommunicating volcanoes, and of which the interiors, being always active, are evidently preparing its ruin. These two volcanoes are those of the Lagonne-ed-Taal and of Monte Albay. When one burns, the other smokes. I shall speak later on of the former of these volcanoes, which, to me at least, appeared a most singular one.

Until the shocks from the volcanoes shall decide its fate, Manilla remains the capital of the Spanish establishments in the Philippines. Here reside the Governor, who is called the Captain-General and President of the Royal Audience. Don Simon de Auda filled this office when I arrived at Manilla. This Governor had previously been a member of the Royal Audience, and when the English, at the end of the last war, took Manilla,[1] he escaped from the city before the surrender, placed himself at the head of the Indians of the province of Pampague, and, without regard to the capitulation of the city, he is said to have succeeded in confining the English within their conquest, starving equally the conquerors and the conquered. Noticing that the Chinese established outside the city walls were furnishing provisions to English and Spaniards alike, he butchered them, putting more than ten thousand to the sword. It seemed to me however that the Spaniards in general considered the efforts of this councillor to be more harmful than advantageous to the welfare of the Spanish colony. The English, harassed by the Indians under Don Simon de Auda, had on their part armed and raised other provinces of Luzon, so as to oppose Indian to Indian, and this sort of civil war did more harm to the colony than even the capture of Manilla by the English.

However this may be, Don Simon de Auda returned to Spain after the peace, was rewarded for his zeal by being made Privy Councillor of Castile, and was sent back to Manilla as Governor-General of the

Fig. 20.

---

[1] Manilla was taken by assault by the English on 6th October, 1762. A full account of the capture is to be found in the "London Gazette" of 19th April, 1763, which contains General Draper's account of the siege. The land force employed was 2300; the fleet was unable to act, owing to bad weather.

Philippines. Since his arrival in his province he has started a number of important projects, but difficult to be carried out at one and the same time. He has started considerable fortifications in various parts of the city, very large barracks, dykes at the mouth of the river, a powder mill, smelting furnaces and forges to work the iron mines, and a number of other useful works, which might have succeeded better had they been started in due succession.

The Philippine Archipelago contains fourteen principal islands, the government of which is divided into twenty-seven provinces, which are governed by *alcades* under the orders of the Governor-Captain-General. All these islands are thickly populated, the estimated population being about three million. These islands extend from the tenth to the twenty-third degree N. latitude, and vary in breadth from about forty leagues at the north head of Luzon up to two hundred leagues from the south of the S.E. point of Mindanao, to the S.W. point of Paragoa. They are all fertile and rich in natural products. But although the Spaniards have been established here for more than two hundred years, they have not yet succeeded in making themselves masters of the islands. They have no foothold on Paragoa, which is almost eighty leagues long, nor on the adjacent small islands; they only possess a few acres on the big island of Mindanao, which is two hundred leagues in circumference, nor are they yet fully acquainted with the interior of the Island of Luzon, where they have their chief settlement, namely, the city of Manilla. Luzon is the largest of these islands, being a hundred and forty leagues long from Cape Bojador to Bulusan Point, which

FIG. 21.

is the most northerly point, and about forty leagues broad. In the northern part of Luzon, near the province of Ilocos, there are some aborigines with whom the Spaniards have

never been able to establish communication. It is believed
that these people are the descendants of Chinese, who, having
been shipwrecked on these shores, have established themselves
in the mountains of this part of the island. It is said that some
Indians know the routes by which access is gained to this
people, and that they have been well received by them; but
it is in the interest of these Indians to withhold the knowledge
from the Spaniards, on account of their great trade profits with
these people, who lack many things and have only provisions
and gold.

Generally speaking, when the Spaniards established themselves
in the Philippines, these islands were inhabited by two varieties
of man,—by the aborigines, mostly black, and by the Malays, of
reddish hue. The former inhabited, and still occupy the forests,
the mountains, and the centre of the islands; they are still wild,
and the Spaniards up to now have not been able to subdue nor
to civilize them. The latter were established along the coasts,
and were colonies formerly transplanted from Sumatra, Malacca,
Borneo and other Malay islands. These latter, in taking the
country, have driven the aborigines into the interior. It was
these inhabitants of the shores that the Spaniards subdued on
arrival, and whose missionaries have converted them to Christianity. These islanders possessed a government, a civilization,
and some arts, and they had kings whose families the Spaniards
destroyed one by one. They have preserved their old language,
and there are only a few Indians in the neighbourhood of
Manilla who speak Spanish. The missionaries on arriving in
the country are first of all obliged to learn the Indian tongue,
which varies according to the different islands. Two different
languages are distinguished, the others being only dialects, the
Tagale language, which is that spoken in Luzon and the adjacent
islands, and the *Bissaïe*, which is the language of the northern
islanders. There are many varieties among the inhabitants of
these islands.[1] At the south of Luzon, Negro Island is so called

[1] This division of the people into that of Tagala and of Bissaya (more correctly
Vissaya) is a very rough and ready one, and, according to our present knowledge,
not accurate. The Tagalas are a very important branch of the Malays, and the

on account of the nature of its inhabitants, whose hair is woolly, and who speak a language which is not met with outside their country. In the neighbouring islands the Spaniards met with men who tatued the body like nearly all the inhabitants of the South Seas as far as New Zealand. It seems that all these people were good navigators, and that various occurrences in the course of navigation have carried them from one island to another, and have mixed them up in a singular manner. It sometimes still happens that crafts are brought by storms to the southern portion of the Philippine Archipelago, containing men who are complete savages, whom it has been impossible to civilize, who speak a language which has no affinity with any language spoken in the Philippines, and whose habitat is not discoverable.

I had an opportunity of seeing some aboriginal savages of Luzon, whom some Spanish Indians had brought in of their own free will.[1] They were very black, with woolly hair, short in stature, but robust and sinewy, and very ugly. Their whole clothing consisted in a girdle of bark, feather bracelets on the forearm, a crown of feathers on the head, like all the savages of the South Seas, a quiver full of arrows on the back and a bow in the hand. They looked very wild, and were much astonished with all that they saw. Accustomed to the silence of the forest, the slightest noise seemed to alarm them, and they were continually looking about in the most uneasy manner. The Spaniards treated them well, but it seemed to me that they preferred their liberty to all the beautiful presents in silk and cotton clothing which the Governor-General gave them. The habits of these savages vary according to the different islands. In some every family lives together, and forms a small society separated from all the rest of humanity; in others every individual lives alone in the forests with his mate. Amongst the former there are some who construct huts in the centre of clumps of trees,

Vissayas a lesser but still important branch of the same. Prof. Blumentritt (Versuch einer Ethnographie der Philipinen, Ergänzungsheft 67 Petermann's Mitth. 1882) has given a very complete description of the natives (aboriginals and others) inhabiting this group.

[1] The aborigines are described by Blumentritt as mentioned above.

where they retire at night time, and often change the site. The Spaniards thought for a long time that there lived on the island of Mindoro a tribe of savages who had tails like monkeys, but after many inquiries this belief was found to be false.[1] This old mistake proves, nevertheless, that in the early days of the discovery the Spaniards were struck with the varieties of the human race they met with in this Archipelago.

The Indians subdued by the Spaniards are very swarthy; they are generally short, with very glossy hair, flat face, eyes something like the Chinese, and the nose short and flattened. The mixture of Indians with Spaniards and Chinese has produced many mestizos, so that in the neighbourhood of Manilla the Indians no longer resemble those at a distance, being very much whiter, and one sees amongst the Indian female population young girls who are as white and as pretty as Spaniards, and others who have all the traits of the Chinese. There are very few European

---

[1] If I read Prof. Terrien de Lacouperie aright (Formosa Notes, Journ. Roy. Asiatic Society, Vol. XIX. Part IV. July, 1887, p. 453), when he refers to the reports of the tailed men of Formosa, he appears to think that because among the Naga tribes men are said to have been discovered so late as the year "1873 with tails about eighteen inches long, made of wood," etc., the old report from Formosa may yet be verified, and supposing the report be verified, its author will then be favoured by posterity with a belief denied him by his contemporaries. But on this subject it will be as well to repeat Dr. Tylor's remarks: "European travellers have tried to rationalize the stories of tailed men which they meet with in Africa and the East. Thus Dr. Krapf points to a leather appendage worn behind from the girdle by the Wakamba, and remarks: 'It is no wonder that people say there are men with tails in the interior of Africa,' and other writers have called attention to hanging mats or waist-cloths, fly-flappers, or artificial tails worn for ornament, as having made their wearers liable to be mistaken at a distance for tailed men. But these apparently silly myths have often a real ethnological significance, deeper at any rate than such a trivial blunder. When an ethnologist meets in any district with the story of tailed men, he ought to look for a despised tribe of aborigines, outcasts, or heretics, living near or among a dominant population, who look upon them as beasts, and furnish them with tails accordingly. Although the aboriginal Miau-tsze, or 'children of the soil,' come down from time to time into Canton to trade, the Chinese still firmly believe them to have short tails like monkeys; the half-civilized Malays describe the ruder forest tribes as tailed men; the Moslem nations of Africa tell the same story of the Niam-Niam of the interior. The outcast race of the Cagots, about the Pyrennees, were said to be born with tails; and in Spain the mediæval super-stition still survives that the Jews have tails, like the devil, as they say" (Primitive Culture, 2nd ed. vol. i. pp. 383-4).

women to be seen at Manilla. The Spaniards have taken Indian women to wife, and the children produced by these marriages have in the second generation turned out as white as Spaniards.

Through all these times the Indians have been well treated by their conquerors, who have not been allowed to make slaves of them. They have thus preserved their original Malay clothes, with a few changes in the cut of the sarong, which is slightly European in form. Their dress consists of a large pair of drawers, in blue or crimson silk, and a shirt, generally of Chinese linen very fine and very white. This shirt, which hangs over the drawers like a tunic, is very often embroidered.[1]

[1] Dr. F. Jagor's Travels in the Philippines will be found an interesting work for those who would care to know something of life in these islands.

THE END OF CROZET'S VOYAGE.

APPENDIX I.

APPENDIX I.

A.—REMARKS BY L'ABBÉ ROCHON.

"In his account of the murder of the Frenchmen in New Zealand, M. Crozet does not give any explanation as to the cause of this unhappy affair. It is, however, quite impossible to conceive the existence of monsters who would, in cold blood and without any provocation, murder strangers, to whom they had extended their hospitality. I know well enough that these savages are cannibals, but there is a great difference between the exercise of this execrable custom of eating up their enemies and the treason of which they are accused.[1]

"Europeans! these savages know the superiority of your arms and their own impotence to punish you, for your unjust acts, otherwise than by surprise. Their perfidious caresses, instead of seducing you, should keep you on the alert. Is it natural, is it possible, that strangers, whose presence astonishes and intimidates them, should gain the affections of a people in the course of a single month, even when the former do not in any way abuse their powers? This reflection alone should have sufficed to save M. Marion. But where are the men who are able to appreciate justly

---

[1] The good Abbé appears to think that in no case would the natives have been the aggressors. But John Rutherford tells us that the vessel on which he escaped from his ten years' captivity among the Maories was to have been taken, without provocation, by the Maories. His words are: "The chiefs now consulted together, and resolved that, if the ship came in, they would take her and murder the crew. Next morning she was observed to be much nearer than she had been the night before; but the chiefs were still afraid that she would not come in, and therefore agreed that I should be sent on board on purpose to decoy her to the land, which I promised to do" (Prof. Craik's The New Zealanders, in Library of Entertaining Knowledge, p. 275).

what they are told from the moment their vanity is flattered and their smallest whim gratified. The unfortunate M. Marion, who was received with every mark of veneration and welcome for thirty-three days, was very far from imagining that he was giving up himself, as well as part of his crew, to the irreconcilable enemies of Europeans. We must acknowledge that these people had to revenge themselves for the very severe treatment they had suffered at the hands of a French ship, commanded by M. de Surville, two years before the arrival of M. Marion at this island. Here are the facts. On his voyage from Pondichery to Peru, M. de Surville touched at New Zealand, and, in hopes of re-establishing the health of his crew, as well as of obtaining fresh provisions, he dropped anchor in a bay S. lat. 34° 41'.

"When M. de Surville went ashore, a chief came to him in his gig, and boarding it in confidence, and with a friendly disposition, asked M. de Surville for his gun. The latter only gave him his sword. The chief immediately ran to show it to a body of Indians which stood at some distance from the shore, and seemed alarmed at M. de Surville's numerous following. The Indians were armed, and held dog-skins and bundles of grass in their hands, and which they continually raised and lowered. The chief in an excited and loud voice seemed to allay their fears, and from that moment a trade was established between the people and the vessel's crew, which brought useful refreshments for the re-establishment of the health of the latter. Unfortunately this trade only lasted from the 17th to the 31st December, 1769. The removal of a boat was the cause of the rupture of the bond of friendship between the people and the Europeans. After a violent gale, which he experienced on this coast, M. de Surville noticed one of his boats stranded on the shore; but when he found time to send to fetch it, all that could be found was the rope and the trail of the boat which had been dragged into and hidden in some creek,—for the trail was followed without success. M. de Surville, wishing to punish the islanders for taking away his boat, made signs to some Indians who were near their canoes, to come to him. One of them ran to him, and was immediately arrested and taken on board; the other Indians fled, and one

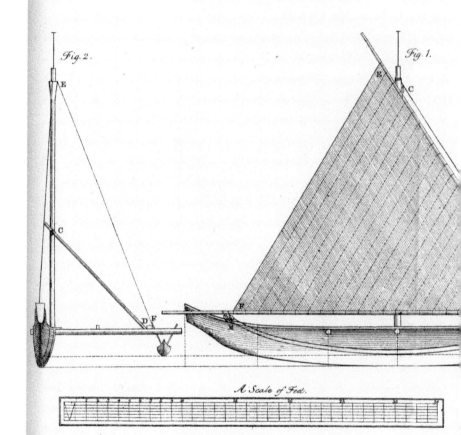

Fig. 2.

Fig. 1.

A Scale of Feet.

Flying Proa, taken at the Ladrone Islands. [AFTER ANSON.]

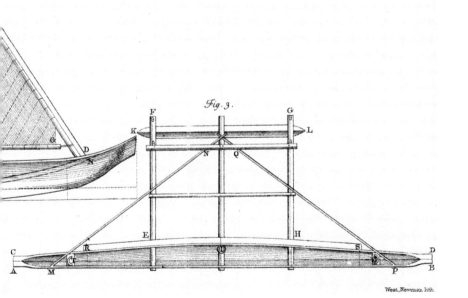

Fig. 3.

of their canoes was taken and the others burned; their huts were also set fire to, and thus having brought terror and desolation to this village, M. de Surville left the island, without foreseeing that the terrible chastisement he had inflicted would have the saddest consequences for all those Europeans who should have the misfortune to follow him. The Indian who was taken captive was named *Naginoui*; he was recognized by the ship's surgeon as a chief who had generously placed his hut at the disposal of the crew's sick hands, and of having given them every help and food in his power, without wishing to receive the slightest reward. And it should be well noted that he gave this assistance at a very critical time; for, on account of the violence of the wind, the boat which was taking the sick on board was obliged to anchor at this chief's village for the three days that the storm lasted.[1] It would no doubt have been possible to obtain from this Indian some information regarding the products of his country and the customs of his countrymen; but the only reference we find in the ship's log is one giving the date of the Indian's death on the 12th March, 1770, while in sight of the Island of Juan Fernandez.

" May we here be permitted to record reflections which draw from us an expression of feeling we are unable to suppress.

" Geographical knowledge and commercial advantages in these distant countries are, it seems, even in our times, bought at the price of human life. It is in ranging the earth that we learn to know it, and it is in hopes of getting a few more superfluities for Europe that we water the soil which produces them with the blood of its inhabitants. We forget that the land inhabited by these savages belongs to them quite as much as the land we inhabit belongs to us. They are almost similar to children, without weapons, without light; and if these children, to whom property of any kind is almost unknown, commit any theft, the importance of which they do not understand, we employ violence

---

[1] The forbearance of this chief may be gauged from the fact that it was customary amongst the Maories to make lawful prizes of all shipwrecks (B. Burns' Brief Narrative of New Zealand Chief, Kendal, 1848, p. 17).

to force them to denounce the guilty party. If we are unable to
obtain this knowledge by violence, we make chance reprisals; and
often, as we have just seen, these reprisals fall on the heads of
those savages who fear European barbarism least, on those who
have treated us generously, on those who think they are right in
relying on our gratitude, that feeling which all nations agree
in regarding as sacred. If the savages appear round our
buildings in numbers large enough to cause anxiety, they are
fired upon, and by the death of a few of their countrymen, they
are taught the power of our fire-arms; then, finally wounded by
these outrages, they make use of treachery, the sole defence
remaining them in their weakness, in order to disgust those
Europeans who come troubling their rest, and their vengeance
knows no mercy. We call them treacherous and cowards,
because they do not come forward and attack artillery and
bayonets with wooden clubs and arrows pointed with fish-bones.

"Europeans are much too strong, and savages much too weak,
for us to look upon the latter as the aggressors. Europeans,
who dress so very much alike, who have the same sort of ships,
the same weapons, and more especially the same general customs,
appear to them as one and the same nation. French, English,
Dutch and Spaniards are often punished for one another, and
perhaps up to now no one has really deserved to have been mistaken by the savages for belonging to any other nation than to
that of the first oppressors.

"Europeans have no right to offer violence to savages except
in procuring what is necessary, and except they are refused the
necessary in exchange for what they offer; but such refusal has
not yet been met with. They ought all the more to be indulgent
towards savages, to treat them with justice, and even to be lenient
towards them, because savages have not the light to see the
extent of the evil they may do. Further, it is the Europeans
who go in quest of them, who expose them to the temptation
of committing the crimes, and who themselves go prepared to
commit all the cruel deeds which may become necessary. Hence
although they may only do that which is necessary in self-defence,
it can never be said that they are innocent.

"What have the voyages, so much glorified by Europeans, brought to these shores? A few more crimes than already existed, and always avenged by fresh crimes, and for which a few useful animals, or a few seeds left by Europeans are, after all, but a poor expiation, and which will not compensate, for a long time, the evil the Europeans have done, nor the contagion Europeans have spread."

B.—Native Accounts of the Massacre.

Dr. Thomson, after giving a very condensed account of the massacre, continues: "Such is the French account of Marion's massacre; the native version I accidentally heard on a singular occasion. During the winter quarter of 1851, the French corvette *L'Alcmène*, thirty-two guns, Commander Count d'Harcourt, was totally wrecked, and ten lives lost, on the west coast of New Zealand, the opposite side of the island, but only fifty miles distant from the place of Marion's massacre. As several men were severely wounded when the ship foundered, the Governor requested me to go and assist their transit across the country to Auckland. When so employed, I awoke one night, and saw a crowd of New Zealanders talking earnestly around a fire. There were then upwards of a hundred French sailors, and nearly two hundred natives, plunged in sleep in the open air all about. Hearing the name of Marion mentioned, I pretended to sleep, and listened to the conversation. From many words, I gathered that, long ago, two vessels commanded by Marion, belonging to the same nation as the shipwrecked sailors, visited the Bay of Islands, and that a strong friendship sprang up between both races; and that they planted the garlic, which flavours the milk, butter and flesh of cows fed in that district. Before the Wewis [*oui-oui-s*], as the French are now called, departed, they violated sacred places, cooked food with tapued wood, and put two chiefs in irons; that, in revenge, their ancestors killed Marion and several of his crew, and in the same spirit the French burned villages and shot many New Zealanders.

" From inquiries made on the spot in 1853, the above narrative and the reason for Marion's murder are, I believe, correct. No man was then alive at the Bay of Islands who had witnessed the affair, and only two old men were acquainted with the particulars of it, although his name was familiar to all. According to the native story, the French, not they, were the aggressors" (The Story of New Zealand, London, 1859, vol. i. pp. 234–5).

Major Richard A. Cruise (Journ. New Zealand, London, 1824, p. 44) gives the following account of the massacre, from the Maori side, fifty years after its occurrence:

"During the time the gentlemen were rowing to the shore, Kokro pointed out the spot where Captain Cook had been attacked by the natives; and gave a minute detail of the massacre of the crew of Marion's ship. He said that the natives, exasperated against the French Captain for having burned two of their villages, determined on revenge; and concealing every hostile disposition towards him and his people, pointed out a place to haul the seine, and offered to assist the sailors in doing so. The arrangement of the plot accorded with the treachery of the proffered kindness. Next to every white man was placed a New-Zealander; and when all hands were busy pulling the net, a sudden and furious attack was made upon the unsuspecting and defenceless Europeans, and every one of them was murdered."

It will be observed that neither of these accounts agree as to the cause of the attack on the Frenchmen; Major Cruise says it was due to the destruction of two Maori villages, and Dr. Thomson ascribes it to violation of sacred places, etc.

It is, of course, only natural that the Maories should maintain that the French were the aggressors, but Englishmen, above all men, before blaming their neighbours, should bear in mind their own difficulties in the South Seas.

APPENDIX II.

Anson's Description of the Outriggers of the Marianne Islanders. (Anson's Voyages, London, 4to. 1748, pp. 340–342.) See accompanying Plate.

"The name of flying proa given to these vessels is owing to the swiftness with which they sail. Of this the Spaniards assert such stories as appear altogether incredible to those who have never seen these vessels move, nor are they the only people who relate these extraordinary tales of their celerity. For those who shall have the curiosity to inquire at the dock at Portsmouth, about a trial made there some years since with a very imperfect one built at that place, will meet with accounts not less wonderful than any the Spaniards have related. However, from some rude estimations made by us of the velocity with which they crossed the horizon at a distance, while we lay at Tinian, I cannot help believing, that with a brisk trade-wind they will run near twenty miles an hour; which, though greatly short of what the Spaniards report of them, is yet a prodigious degree of swiftness. But let us give a distinct idea of its figure.

"The construction of this proa is a direct contradiction to the practice of all the rest of mankind. For as the rest of the world make the head of their vessels different from the stern, but the two sides alike; the proa, on the contrary, has her head and stern exactly alike, but her two sides very different; the side intended to be always the lee side being flat;[1] whilst the windward side is built rounding, in the manner of other vessels. And, to prevent her oversetting, which from her small breadth, and the straight run of her leeward side would, without this precaution, infallibly happen, there is a frame laid out from her

---

[1] Crozet says the exact reverse of this. See p. 94.

to windward to the end of which is fastened a log, fashioned into the shape of a small boat, and made hollow. The weight of the frame is intended to balance the proa, and the small boat is by its buoyancy (as it is always in the water) to prevent her oversetting to windward, and this frame is usually called an outrigger. The body of the proa (at least of that we took) is made of two pieces of wood joined endways, and sewed together with bark, for there is no iron used in her construction. She is about two inches thick at the bottom, which at the gunwale is reduced to less than one. The dimensions of each part will be better known from the uprights and plans contained in the annexed plate, which were drawn from an exact mensuration; these I shall endeavour to explain as minutely and distinctly as I can.

"Fig. 1 represents the proa with her sail set, as she appears when seen from the leeward.

"Fig. 2 is a view of her from the head, with the outrigger to the windward.

"Fig. 3 is the plan of the whole; where AB is the lee side of the proa; CD the windward side; EFGH the outrigger, or frame, laid out to windward; KL the boat at the end of it; MNPQ two braces from the head and stern to steady the frame; RS a thin plank placed to windward, to prevent the proa from shipping water and for a seat to the Indian who bales, and sometimes goods are carried upon it; I is the part of the middle outrigger, on which the mast is fixed. The mast itself is supported (Fig. 2) by the shore, CD, and by the shroud, EF, and by two stays, one of which may be seen in Fig. 1, marked CD, the other is hid by the sail. The sail, EFG, in Fig. 1, is made of matting, and the mast, yard, boom, and outriggers are all made of bamboo. The heel of the yard is always lodged in one of the sockets, T or V, Fig. 3, according to the tack the proa goes on; and when she alters her tack, they bear away a little to bring her stern up to the wind, then, by easing the halyard and raising the yard, and carrying the heel of it along the lee side of the proa, they fix it in the opposite socket; whilst the boom at the same time, by letting fly the sheet, M, and haling the sheet, N, Fig. 1, shifts into a contrary situation to what it had before, and that which was the stern of the proa now becomes the head, and she is trimmed on the other tack. When it is necessary to reef or furl the sail, this is done by rolling it round the boom. The proa generally carries six or seven Indians; two of which are placed in the head or stern, who steer the vessel alternately with a paddle, according to the tack she goes on, he in the stern being the steersman; the other Indians are employed either in baling out the water which she accidentally ships, or in setting and trimming the sail. From the description of these vessels it is sufficiently obvious, how dexterously they are fitted for ranging this collection of islands called the Ladrones. Since these islands bear nearly all N. and S. of each other, and are all within the limits of the trade wind, the proas, by sailing most excellently on a wind, and with either end foremost, can run from one of these islands to the other and back again only by shifting the sail, without ever putting about; and by the flatness of their leeside and their small breadth, they are capable of lying much nearer the wind than any other vessel hitherto known, and thereby have an advantage which no vessels that go large can ever pretend to. The advantage I mean is that of running with a velocity nearly as great, and perhaps sometimes greater, than that with which the wind blows."

[Although the drawing shows pulley blocks in use on this proa, there is no reference to them in the text, nor do the islanders appear to know their use.]

APPENDIX III.

A BRIEF REFERENCE TO THE LITERATURE RELATING TO NEW ZEALAND.

By JAMES R. BOOSÉ, LIBRARIAN OF THE ROYAL COLONIAL INSTITUTE.

Unlike the literature relating to China, when in the year 513 B.C. during the dynasty of T'sin, in order to eradicate the traditions of the subjugated kingdoms, it was ordered "that all the records in charge of the historiographers be burned, and that those who make mention of the past so as to blame the present be put to death along with their relatives; and that whosoever shall not have burned their books within thirty days of the issuing of the ordinance, be branded and sent to labour for four years on the Wall," the literature regarding New Zealand has fortunately not suffered in a similar manner. It is therefore possible to obtain an unbroken record of the history of the Colony from such works as have from time to time been issued from the press.

In this short chapter it is in no way proposed to set forth a complete bibliography of works relating to New Zealand, more especially as there is in existence the excellent one compiled by Mr. J. Collier, Librarian of the General Assembly Library at Wellington, which was published two years ago, and which deals in a most complete manner with the various epochs in the history of New Zealand. Taking into consideration the existence of this valuable work, it is simply the writer's intention to submit a brief reference to the principal publications relating to New Zealand which have appeared since our first acquaintance with the Colony to the present time.

Although the actual settlement of New Zealand is an event of recent date, the literature connected with it is remarkably extensive and varied. The first and by far the most arduous duty of the writer was to determine upon a plan of his work, selecting and excluding names, determining their relative value, and deciding what proportion of the space at his command could be spared for individual mention. An idea of the extent of this work may be gained when it is stated that the bibliography of Mr. Collier occupies 235 pages of closely printed matter relating to events in the history of the Colony extending from the year 1642 to 1889. As further evidence of the immensity of this literature a bibliography appeared in the second volume of Dr. Thomson's "Story of New Zealand," published in 1859, which the author states contains "Ninety volumes and two hundred pamphlets, and nearly a hundredweight of Parliamentary Papers." Having summarized this vast array of literature, it will be necessary, in order to consider the various stages in the history of New Zealand, to divide the subject into five periods, mentioning only the principal works regarding each as a guide to the student of New Zealand affairs. These periods have been: (1) The discovery and early visits of the Europeans, (2) The period of Civilization, including accounts of the native inhabitants, together with the labours of the Missionaries, (3) The Colonization of the Country, (4) The New Zealand War, and (5) The History of the Colony generally, including its gradual progress and its present position as an important portion of the British Empire.

Setting aside the claims set up for the discovery of New Zealand anterior to the voyage of Abel Jansen Tasman, but which have no substantiation, we find that the first account of that Navigator's discoveries was published in Dutch during the year 1674, and during that ever memorable century which has been appropriately termed the Century of Companies, on account of the British, the French, the Spaniards, and the Dutch, having simultaneously recognized the great principle of co-operation in the furtherance of commercial enterprise. Although Tasman did not land upon the shores of New Zealand, he nevertheless proved to the world the existence in the Southern Seas of an important territory. It is an extraordinary fact, however, that the only account of this voyage, in the performance of which Tasmania and New Zealand were discovered, that the world possessed for more than a century after its termination, was a curtailed abridgment previously referred to, which was published at

Amsterdam, and an abstract of a more extended kind accompanied with charts and views, included in Valentyn's Dutch work on the East Indian Possessions of the Company. In 1771, however, a manuscript journal of Tasman's, written by his own hand, was brought to England by "a person unknown," and offered for sale to Sir Joseph Banks, who, having established its authenticity, purchased it, and subsequently lent it to Captain (afterwards Admiral) Burney, who embodied it in the third volume of his important Collection of Voyages to the South Seas. At Sir Joseph Banks's death his library was bequeathed to the British Museum, where Tasman's original journal is still to be found. Doubts havng been raised as to the genuineness of the journal, Captain Burney, in the introduction to his work, discusses at length the question of its authenticity, and conclusively proves that it possesses every mark of originality. The literature describing the exploits of the later discoverers would require a volume for a mere summary, but the following collections of voyages, in addition to those of Burney, may be regarded as bearing upon the discovery of and early voyages to New Zealand. The collections of Dr. John Harris (1764), M. Charles de Brosses' Histoire des Navigations aux Terres Australes (1756), Callander's Terra Australis Cognita, or Voyages to the Southern Hemisphere (1766–68), which is an English translation of the preceding work with additions, and Alexander Dalrymple's Collection, published in 1770–71. Coming to a later date, the next work of importance, and one which has ever held the highest position in the history of maritime discovery, was the account of the voyage of Captain Cook, who visited New Zealand after leaving the Society Islands in 1769, published in Dr. Hawkesworth's Collection of Voyages (1773), and for which work the compiler received from Government £6000. For the remaining works dealing with this period may be mentioned the voyage of M. de Surville, and that of M. Marion du Fresne, which was compiled by the Abbé Rochon from the papers of M. Crozet, Marion's Lieutenant.

Turning now to the second period, viz. the Period of Civilization, a large number of works may with advantage be consulted.

During this period religion was a very potent influence in the settlement of the country. It bestowed upon New Zealand the services of a zealous, devoted band of missionaries, who, with unfaltering courage, forced their way into the interior. The accounts of their experiences, together with descriptions of the aboriginal inhabitants, form a large collection, but the following may be mentioned: John Savage's Account of New Zealand (1807); Nicholas's Narrative of a Voyage to New Zealand, 1817; Kendall and Lee's Grammar and Vocabulary of the Language of New Zealand, 1820; Jules de Blosseville's Mémoire Géographique sur la Nouvelle Zélande, 1826. The New Zealanders, written by G. L. Craik, and containing the history of John Rutherford, a sailor, supposed to have been detained among the natives for a considerable number of years, of which work part is stated to have been written by Lord Brougham. Yate's account of New Zealand, and of the formation of the Church Missionary Society's Mission in the Northern Island (1835), the contents being the result of personal observation during a residence there of seven years. J. S. Polack's New Zealand: a Narrative of Travels and Adventures (1838), together with a second work by the same Author, entitled Manners and Customs of the New Zealanders, published in 1840. In 1841 Dieffenbach's New Zealand and its Native Population appeared, under the auspices of the Aborigines Protection Society. W. Browns, New Zealand and its Aborigines (1845). The New Zealanders Illustrated, by George French Angas, containing sixty coloured plates, with descriptions, appeared in 1847, followed in the same year by Savage Life and Scenes in Australia and New Zealand, by the same author. Buddle's Aborigines of New Zealand (1851); Edward Shortland's Southern Districts of New Zealand (1854), which was compiled from the notes of a journal written during part of the years 1843-4, during which the author was employed in the service of the Colonial Government as a Protector of the Aborigines, and Traditions and Superstitions of the New Zealanders (1856) by the same author. In 1855 one of the most important books in connection with the History of the Aborigines of New Zealand was published, having been written by Sir George

9

Grey, and entitled Polynesian Mythology and Ancient Traditional History of the New Zealand Race. For studying the ancient history of the Maori no better work could be consulted. In the preface the author describes how he came to collect the legends. It may be mentioned that Sir George Grey at this period made a collection of New Zealand Books and Pamphlets to the extent of 311 Printed Volumes and 223 Manuscripts, all in the Maori language, which were subsequently presented by him to the South African Public Library at Cape Town, where they at present are located, and form part of the Grey Collection. Owing to the generosity of Sir George Grey, the Auckland Public Library possesses a valuable collection of South African literature, which would doubtless prove of great value to the Cape Library. In commenting upon his various gifts to these two libraries, Sir George Grey appears to have recognized that the donations should have been reversed; for he says in the preface to the second edition of Polynesian Mythology, " I must seem to have made an injudicious arrangement regarding the place of deposit of great historical treasures." If it were possible for those two libraries to effect an exchange, the residents of both Colonies would benefit by the possession of many valuable documents regarding the early history of their individual portions of the Empire.

Another work which should not be omitted from a selection of works under this heading is Judge Maning's Old New Zealand; a tale of the good old times, which was published in 1863, and contains a description of old Maori life and manners. This book was reprinted in 1876, with an introduction by the Earl of Pembroke. Nor must mention be omitted of Mr. John White's works, which include Te Rou, or the Maori at Home (1874), and his complete and exhaustive work consisting of four volumes, the first of which appeared in 1887. The work was compiled under the direction of the Government of New Zealand. There are, of course, many other works which may with advantage be referred to, including those of the Rev. R. Taylor, W. Colenso, the Rev. J. Buller, the Rev. Dr. Williams, Bishop of Waiapu, Lady Martin, and Mr. J. C. Johnston, all of which contain valuable information with regard to the customs and habits of the Maoris and the history of the various missionary efforts in the Colony.

In dealing with the third period, it will be necessary to refer to the time known as that of the Company period, during which the colonisation of the Colony took place upon an extended scale. A large number of works have found their way into circulation, but the following may be considered the more important: J. W. Lang's New Zealand in 1839, which contains four letters addressed to Lord Durham as Chairman of the New Zealand Land Company, in which he urged that the Company ought to make way for a National Colony, and made the extraordinary declaration that the church missionaries had actually been the principals in the grand conspiracy of the European inhabitants to rob and plunder the natives of their land. A work entitled The Colonisation of New Zealand, being a brief history of The New Zealand Company of London (1840); The Reports of the Directors of the New Zealand Company (1840), which gives a sketch of the Associations merged in the Company and of the formation of the Company, with a statement of its principles; A Narrative of a Residence in New Zealand, by Charles Heaphy, who was Draftsman to the New Zealand Company (1842); An Account of the Settlements of the New Zealand Company, by the Hon. H. W. (afterwards Lord) Petre (1842); Petition of the New Zealand Company presented to the House of Commons, by Joseph Somes, M.P., the Governor of the Company (1845), which contains a history of the Colony up to that date; E. J. Wakefield's Adventures in New Zealand from 1839–44, together with a volume of fifteen coloured plates; The New Zealand Question, by L. A. Chamerovzow (1848); Edward Gibbon Wakefield's View of the Art of Colonisation (1849), which contains an exposition of the principles on which the New Zealand Company's and the Canterbury Association's Settlements were founded; The Canterbury Papers (1851) consisting of information concerning the principles, objects, plans and proceedings of the founders of the Settlement of Canterbury; W. Swainson's New Zealand, consisting of Lectures on the

Colonisation of New Zealand (1856); C. W. Adams' A Spring in the Canterbury Settlement; and F. Fuller's Five Years' Residence in New Zealand (1859), with Observations on Colonisation.

The next period, and one which may be referred to with regret, relates to the war in New Zealand, and among other works the following supply sufficient information on all questions regarding its cause and the operations of the contending forces during the years 1860–61. The first work published upon this subject was that of the Rev. T. Gilbert, entitled New Zealand Settlers and Soldiers, or the War in Taranaki. Sir J. E. Alexander issued, in 1862, a work entitled Incidents of the Maori War, and ten years later the same author gave a detailed account of the war under the title of Bush Fighting in New Zealand, in the preface to which he states that he has introduced the name of every officer, non-commissioned officer, or private sentinel, soldier or sailor he could discover who is mentioned in any despatch or report of a creditable action. Swainson's New Zealand and the War also appeared in 1862. In 1864 the present Under Secretary of State for India published an interesting account of the war, entitled The Maori King, or the Story of our Quarrel with the Natives of New Zealand. At that time Sir John Gorst was in the service of the New Zealand Government as Commissioner of the Waikato District. Two years later a book appeared under the title of The War in New Zealand, written by William Fox, whose long and valuable services to the Colony have been recognized by Her Majesty by the bestowal upon him of a Knight Commandership of the Order of St. Michael and St. George. The preface to this work contains so full a description of the services of this eminent Colonist that extracts from it are worthy of reproduction. It runs as follows: " I have been a Colonist of New Zealand almost from its foundation as a Colony. I have been a member of the Legislature for many years, and during a great part of the present struggle I filled the offices of Colonial Secretary and Native Minister. I have probably had better opportunities of obtaining accurate information and observing current events in the Colony than any other person. . . . In describing the operations of the military campaigns, I have relied for the main facts chiefly on the despatches of General Cameron or of his subordinate officers who may have reported to him.   I have also referred to the contemporary reports of the correspondents of the local newspapers.   I am myself acquainted, more or less, with all the country in which operations were carried on; and as regards the Northern campaign, I have visited all the places where the principal engagements occurred, many of them several times, and most of them in company of officers who were in the engagements, and described them to me on the spot." The remaining work upon this subject, which may with advantage be consulted, is T. W. Gudgeon's Reminiscences of the War in New Zealand, which was not published until 1879.   The author had exceptional opportunities for gaining information, having held the position of Lieutenant and Quartermaster of the Colonial Forces.

The last and, from a general point of view, the most important, section of this brief chapter is that relating to the history of the Colony in connexion with its rise, progress and present position as one of the most important portions of the Colonial Empire of Great Britain.   The selection of a few of the chief works regarding this subject from the immense stock of literature extending over so long a period is a difficult and arduous undertaking.   The following works, however, may be put forth as dealing with the questions affecting the general history, government, and commercial position of the Colony: Major Cruise's Journal of a Ten Months' Residence in New Zealand (1824); James Busby's Our Colonial Empire and the Case of New Zealand (1866), in which, in addition to dealing with the question of the grant of Responsible Government, the author explains and illustrates the true relations of the British Colonies to the Mother Country; Charles Terry's New Zealand and its Advantages and Prospects as a British Colony (1842); the New Zealand Portfolio, by H. S. Chapman (1843); Ernest Dieffenbach's Travels in New Zealand (1843), which work Hochstetter says comprises numerous geological observations relative to the North Island particularly, and asserts that (in 1867) it was one of the best books on New Zealand; Mr. Brodie's Remarks on the Past and Present of New Zealand (1845); Dr. S. M. D. Martin's New Zealand (1845).   The author of this work was at one time editor of the Auckland Gazette, and was one of the signers of a letter to Lord Stanley, intimating the intention of settlers at the Bay of Islands to emigrate to an island in the Pacific for the purpose of forming a permanent settlement. An Account of the Settlement of New Plymouth, by Charles Hursthouse (1849); G. B. Earp's New Zealand (1853); T. Cholmondeley's Ultima Thule, or Thoughts Suggested by a Residence in New Zealand (1854); E. B. Fitton's New Zealand (1856); C. Hursthouse's New Zealand, the Britain of the South (1857); Dr. George Bennett's Gatherings of a Naturalist in Australasia (1860); Sir William Martin's Taranaki Question (1860); Edwin Hodder's Memoirs of New Zealand Life (1862); F. von Hochstetter's New Zealand; its Physical Geography, Geology, and Natural History (1867); Sir Walter Buller's History of the Birds of New Zealand (1888); Alexander Kennedy's New Zealand (1873): James Adam's Twenty-five Years of Emigrant Life in New Zealand (1874); Alexander Bathgate's Colonial Experiences (1874); A Story of New Zealand Life, published in 1881; the Rev. J. Buller's Forty Years in New Zealand (1878), in the Appendix of which a lecture entitled "New Zealand, the Future England of the Southern Hemisphere," appears; B. Wells' History of Taranaki (1878); Sir J. Hector's Handbook of New Zealand, of which four editions have appeared, extending over the years 1879–1886; John Bathgate's New Zealand, its Resources and Prospects (1880); John Buchanan's Indigenous Grasses of New Zealand (1880); J. Coutts Crawford's Recollections of Travel in New Zealand (1880); Dr. J. Logan Campbell's Poenamo, or Sketches of the Early Days of New Zealand (1881); John Bradshaw's New Zealand as it is (1883); H. Bramall's Mineral Resources of New Zealand (1883); W. S. Green's High Alps of New Zealand (1883); G. W. Rusden's History of New Zealand (1883); G. W. Griffin's New Zealand—Her Commerce and Resources (1884); J. H. Kerry-Nicholls' King Country (1884); W. Gisborne's New Zealand Rulers and Statesmen (1886), which is a biographical history of the Colony from its foundation, written by a former Member of the House of Representatives and a Responsible Minister of the Colony, who in 1888 published a further work entitled The Colony of New Zealand, its History, etc.; The Handbook of New Zealand Mines (1887); J. Bradshaw's New Zealand of To-day (1888); Sir James Hector's Phormium Tenax as a Fibrous Plant (1889); T. Kirk's Forest Flora of New Zealand (1889), containing 157 plates; The Picturesque Atlas of Australasia, edited by Dr. Andrew Garran, which is illustrated with many New Zealand Scenes and accompanying letterpress; Dr. Murray Moore's New Zealand for the Emigrant, Invalid, and Tourist (1890); and Edward Wakefield's New Zealand after Fifty Years (1890).

Such is a brief summary of the principal works which it is suggested may prove of value to the student of New Zealand affairs. It is not, however, in any way intended by the writer to claim that such works only shall be consulted, for there are many, probably of equal importance, which have been omitted solely on account of the limited amount of space available. For instance, there are important publications in pamphlet form containing discussions of special subjects, matters of history, ethnology, and other departments of inquiry incident to the respective portions of the Colony, and descriptive of contemporary adventure and research. It would not be right, however, to close this chapter without referring to the Proceedings of the New Zealand Institute, a society which has rendered invaluable service in diffusing information upon all questions affecting the Colonisation and Progress of the Colony. The several papers included in its proceedings have been contributed by the most eminent men connected with New Zealand, prominent amongst whom may be mentioned Sir James Hector, who has performed the duties of editor since the foundation of the Institute in 1868, and whose long and brilliant efforts in the cause of science have secured for him both fame and honours in this country.

INDEX.

PRINTED BY STEPHEN AUSTIN AND SONS, HERTFORD.

For EU product safety concerns, contact us at Calle de José Abascal, 56–1°,
28003 Madrid, Spain or eugpsr@cambridge.org.

www.ingramcontent.com/pod-product-compliance
Ingram Content Group UK Ltd.
Pitfield, Milton Keynes, MK11 3LW, UK
UKHW012346130625
459647UK00009B/558